History and Philosophy of the Language Sciences

Editor: James McElvenny

In this series:

1. McElvenny, James (ed.). Form and formalism in linguistics.

2. Van Rooy, Raf. Greece's labyrinth of language: A study in the early modern discovery of dialect diversity.

3. Aussant, Émilie & Jean-Michel Fortis. Historical journey in a linguistic archipelago: Case studies on concepts, fields, and commitments.

4. McElvenny, James & Ploder, Andrea. Holisms of communication: The early history of audio-visual sequence analysis.

5. Anderson, Stephen R. Phonology in the Twentieth Century: Second edition, revised and expanded.

6. James McElvenny (ed.). Interviews in the history of linguistics: Volume I.

ISSN (print): 2629-1711

ISSN (electronic): 2629-172X

Interviews in the history of linguistics

Volume I

Edited by

James McElvenny

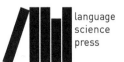

language
science
press

James McElvenny (ed.). 2022. *Interviews in the history of linguistics: Volume I* (History and Philosophy of the Language Sciences 6). Berlin: Language Science Press.

This title can be downloaded at:
http://langsci-press.org/catalog/book/361
© 2022, the authors
Published under the Creative Commons Attribution 4.0 Licence (CC BY 4.0):
http://creativecommons.org/licenses/by/4.0/
ISBN: 978-3-96110-396-6 (Digital)
      978-3-98554-054-9 (Hardcover)

ISSN (print): 2629-1711
ISSN (electronic): 2629-172X
DOI: 10.5281/zenodo.7092391
Source code available from www.github.com/langsci/361
Errata: paperhive.org/documents/remote?type=langsci&id=361

Cover and concept of design: Ulrike Harbort
Typesetting: James McElvenny
Proofreading: Amir Ghorbanpour, Aviva Shimelman, Brett Reynolds, Cathryn A. Yang, Elen Le Foll, Elliott Pearl, George Walkden, Hella Olbertz, Jeroen van de Weijer, Daniela Hanna-Kolbe, Lisa Schäfer, Matthew Windsor, Jean Nitzke, Patricia Cabredo Hofherr, Rebecca Madlener, Rong Chen, Sarah Warchhold, Sean Stalley, Sophie Ellsaeßer, Yvonne Treis,
Fonts: Libertinus, Arimo, DejaVu Sans Mono
Typesetting software: XƎLATEX

Language Science Press
xHain
Grünberger Str. 16
10243 Berlin, Germany
http://langsci-press.org

Storage and cataloguing done by FU Berlin

Freie Universität Berlin

To Luca Dinu,

whose transcripts laid the foundations for this book

Contents

Preface

Over the past two and a half years, the History and Philosophy of the Language Sciences podcast (https://hiphilangsci.net/category/podcast/) has been exploring the history of modern linguistics, from its beginnings in the early nineteenth century up to the present. This volume brings together transcripts of ten interviews from the podcast on topics related to the history of European linguistics.

The transcripts published here diverge in some ways from the broadcast interviews: the interviewees and I have edited the transcripts for clarity and completeness, and to insert all the witty repartee that we have thought of in the meantime. The original audio file of each interview can be found under the DOI link at the bottom of the first page in each chapter.

The podcast consists not only of interviews, but also episodes that take the form of short lectures. These episodes will be published in substantially revised and expanded form in the book *A History of Modern Linguistics*, forthcoming with Edinburgh University Press.

The podcast is ongoing and is constantly branching out into new areas. Further monographs and collected volumes of interviews will appear in the near future.

Hamburg, September 2022   James McElvenny

Chapter 1

Wilhelm von Humboldt

Jürgen Trabant[a] & James McElvenny[b]

[a]Free University of Berlin [b]University of Siegen

JMc: Today we're joined by Jürgen Trabant, Emeritus Professor of Romance Philology at the Free University of Berlin, who'll be talking to us about Wilhelm von Humboldt. Jürgen is the author of numerous works on Humboldt in several languages. You can find a selection of his most significant works in the references list.

So, Jürgen, what would you say is the foundation of Humboldt's philosophy of language? You have written about what you call Humboldt's "anti-semiotics". Could you tell us about what this is and how it fits into the philosophical landscape of Humboldt's time?

JT: Yes, the anti-semiotics of Humboldt is very interesting, and it goes to the very philosophical heart of Humboldt's language philosophy, because he was, on that point, anti-Aristotelian. The semiotic conception of language was for centuries linked to the European reception of the *De Interpretatione* of Aristotle. Aristotle had the idea that languages are pure means of communication, hence signs. Aristotle introduced the term "sign", *semeion*, into the history of language philosophy. The idea was that: Here are the humans. They are everywhere the same, and they think the same everywhere, and they create ideas, their thoughts, universally in the same way. And when they want to communicate those thoughts, they use signs. They use sounds which are signs and which are completely arbitrary, or as Aristotle says, *kata syntheken*.

Hence we have this idea that words and languages are arbitrary signs, which is then taken up by Saussure – but in a different way, by the way. What Humboldt

 Jürgen Trabant & James McElvenny. 2022. Wilhelm von Humboldt. In James McElvenny (ed.), *Interviews in the history of linguistics: Volume I*, 1–12. Berlin: Language Science Press. DOI: 10.5281/zenodo.7096288

and other European thinkers realize, mainly in the seventeenth and eighteenth centuries, is that languages, words are not signs in that way, but that languages in a sense shape thought in different ways. This was a catastrophic insight for the British philosophers – for Bacon, for Locke. They realized that the common languages – or the languages of extra-European people more so – shaped thought in different ways. So the Europeans realized that it was difficult to say what the Christians wanted to communicate in Nahuatl or Otomi, in American languages, and hence they realized that the languages create different thought. And this is the idea Humboldt takes up through Leibniz, mainly, and which he then transforms into his language philosophy and which he transforms also into his linguistic project. The aim of his linguistic project is exactly enquiry into the diversity of human thought. And this is why his title is *Über die Verschiedenheit des menschlichen Sprachbaues, On the Diversity of Human Language Construction*. So I think the anti-semiotics leads us to the very centre of Humboldt's linguistic philosophy.

JMc: OK, and in terms of the immediate philosophical context in which he was working, do you think that Humboldt's thought came out of a particularly German tradition or was it pan-European?

JT: I would say the discovery that different languages create different thought, that was pan-European. But it was mainly in the British world that it was seen as a catastrophic insight because then communication becomes even more difficult than after the Tower of Babel. Now we have really different thought systems, and the German side of it is that Leibniz transformed this idea, this insight, into a celebration of diversity. Leibniz said it's *la merveilleuse variété des opérations de notre esprit*, the marvellous variety of the operations of our spirit, of our mind, and this celebration of diversity is what Humboldt takes up. He was educated by Leibnizian philosophers. His teacher was a Leibnizian, and his earliest education was very much formed by this Leibnizian joy of individualism, of diversity, of the wealth of being diverse. And then, of course, Humboldt became a Kantian, which is another story, but Kant then, in a certain way, is the general background for his construction of a philosophy of language. But I would say the very idea of creating a new linguistics is Leibniz, and it's Herder, and hence it is very German because it's this celebration, this joy of diversity which is the German contribution to linguistics, because only if you see that the languages of the world are different worldviews, that they create different semantics, different insights, then the research into those languages becomes a worthy thing. Otherwise, why would you research languages if they are only means of communication?

JMc: Hans Aarsleff has made the case that Humboldt's time studying in Paris played an important role at least in turning his attention to language, if not in shaping his outlook, but do you think that plays a significant role at all in Humboldt's thinking?

JT: No, I mean, we, the German scholars, researched this for some time. Aarsleff invented this legend, and I think we really found that this was not the case, I mean that Humboldt was not a German ideologist, *un idéologue allemand.* He was 30 years old when he came to Paris, and he was a complete Kantian, and he tried to convince the French philosophers of his Kantian insights. And the idea that Humboldt is a French philosopher is completely absurd, and I think this was proven by years of research into that idea. But what is certainly right is that Humboldt discovered in Paris his linguistic interest, not via *les idéologues*, but via his encounter with the Basque language, so he encountered this very strange language – before that he was, he had already written about language. But then he finds this very strange language, and his question is how can you think in such a strange language, which is completely different from what he knew from the Indo-European languages, and from Hebrew – these were the languages he knew – and then he goes into that strange language. He travels to the Basque country. He travels to his New World, in a certain way, and then he is fascinated by it, by languages, and he becomes a real linguist trying to get into the structure of languages. Then, as you know, his brother brings American languages, American grammars and dictionaries to Rome.

JMc: So Alexander von Humboldt.

JT: Alexander von Humboldt, yes. This is also very important: Alexander brings these twelve books, which I consider to be the very first moment in real comparative descriptive linguistics, so he brings these books to Europe, and Friedrich Schlegel reads them first, and then after Schlegel, because Wilhelm doesn't have the time to read them. But when he has got the time after 1811 and in the 1820s, he studies these books, and he tries to describe those American languages and their really different structural personality.
  I think this is very important, because Humboldt is really not a philosopher from the very beginning. He is a real linguist, and from his linguistics, he goes into philosophy. We have to consider his initial education. When he was young, he was looking for something to do, some contribution he could make. He was not a poet, and he discovered that he was not a philosopher, philosophy was done

by Kant, and he believed in Kant. Kant is his master and the master of Germany. But what he discovered and what he was really good at was anthropology. What is anthropology? Anthropology is the description and the study of the concrete manifestations of humanity – not philosophy, not the universal, but the concrete, historical, particular, individual manifestations of humans. And this is what he starts with first. He goes to Paris in order to write a book on, an anthropological study of France. This is what his project is, and then he discovers languages, and he finds that in the very centre of the *anthropos*, of the human, we have language, language as the creation of thought. And now, when he studies languages, at the same time, he writes or he tries to develop his philosophy.

   If you look at what Humboldt really published – he published very few things during his lifetime, practically only some of his speeches at the Berlin Academy – we often forget the book on the Basque because it's not very Humboldtian. He publishes only eight discourses from the Academy, but he presents I think something like 18 or 17 topics there. So he is 50 years old, when he starts publishing. And what does he publish? He publishes linguistics, linguistic descriptions, grammatical problems on Sanskrit and so on and so forth, on the American languages, and then, of course, at the end of his life, on the Pacific Austronesian languages. So what he presents, really, to the public is linguistic things, but what he does not publish, but what he is working on, is the philosophical part of it, because he has to justify to himself why he is doing this, why he is studying languages. And hence he has to develop a philosophy of language, which is published only after his death, in the first volume of his main work on the Kawi-Sprache.

JMc: OK, so that's a good connection to our next question, which is, how would you say does Humboldt's concrete study of language, of human language and particular languages, relate to his overall philosophy, in particular the distinction that Humboldt makes between the "construction" or the "organism" of a language and its "character"?

JT: Yes, that is a very important question. We first have to say what this opposition is. Studying the construction or the structure, he calls it *den Bau*, and in French he calls it *structure, charpente*, so it's the term "structure" which comes up here. And he says we have to study the structures of languages. He also calls these structures the "organisms". We have to do a systematic study of languages as structures. This is the first step, and then he says this is only the dead skeleton, *das tote Gerippe*, of languages. But languages are not a dead skeleton, languages are spoken. They are action. They are *energeia*. They are activity, and hence to really see what languages are, we have to look at them in action, in speech, in literature. He adds to the description of the construction another chapter on the character. He says if we really want to grasp the very individuality of languages, we have to look into literature, and hence he joined linguistics – and he says *Linguistik* – to philology, *Philologie*. So for him, linguistics, structural linguistics, and the history of that language in its texts are two parts of language study.

What is so interesting in the nineteenth century is that, because this dichotomy in the nineteenth century is very strong, the philologists – so those are the classicists – are immediately against linguistics, because linguistics becomes a natural science, it becomes structural, it becomes very technical, and the philologists, they want to stay with their texts. Humboldt sees both together, structure and texts, and he wants them not to be separate, but two chapters, in a certain way, of language studies. But then, of course, in the nineteenth century, these things get separated. Steinthal is perhaps the last one who tries, again, to put these two together. He has what he called *Stilistik*, stylistics. *Stilistik* is actually the study of the character of languages. But the nineteenth century is not a century of character, but it comes up in the twentieth century and afterwards, so there are linguists who think that language is something living, is an activity, and that we have to study the active usage of language, but I would say this comes in the twentieth century with people like Karl Vossler, with so-called idealism, which is then considered by the linguists of the nineteenth century as non-linguistic.

JMc: So you were saying that Humboldt has these two compartments, the structure and the character. But is it not the case that Humboldt felt that the character was more important than the structure? He calls character the *Schlussstein*, the keystone.

JT: Yes, it's the *Schlussstein*. The final aim would be the description of the character of a language. But he never succeeds in describing the character in his Nahuatl grammar, which is the only grammar he really finished and he really nearly published also, which Manfred Ringmacher only published in the nineties. There, he has a chapter on the character, but the chapter is very weak because he does not have texts. Humboldt does not have Nahuatl texts, or very few, only translations, and hence he can't grasp the character. Hence this chapter on the character is rather deceptive, and when you look for what Humboldt is thinking of when he talks of character, he says we have to study the literature and how the people talk, and then he has one footnote where he refers to a history of Greek literature. He says the history of Greek prose might be a description of the character of the Greek language. It's very hidden, but at the same time, it's also very true, because what is the description of an individual? The scientific description of an individual is his or her story, her history or his history. So there is no definition of an individual, but in order to say scientifically something about an individual, you have to write his or her history. And this, I think, is the wisdom of that footnote in Humboldt, but he himself, he never succeeds in writing such a description of character. He himself writes grammars, descriptions of the dead skeleton, and writes sketches of other American Indian languages.

What is also important to remember is that we only know the linguistic work of Humboldt, because Mueller-Vollmer realized – when he saw the material that was not published – that we have to join Humboldt's linguistic descriptions to his philosophy. Humboldt is known as a philosopher of language, but he was also a real linguist, and he tried to deal with linguistic structure, and the American languages of which he had some knowledge came in grammars which were framed in terms of Latin or Spanish grammar. So you had paradigms like *rosa*, *rosae*, *rosae*, *rosam*, etc., and of course, the Spanish priests who wrote those descriptions followed the Latin, European, Indo-European Spanish grammar, and hence we have descriptions which do not at all render even the individual structure of those languages. So in a certain way, those descriptions even destroy the individuality of the American Indian languages, and Humboldt was very much aware of that problem. What he tried to do in the Nahuatl grammar is to get through those Indo-European descriptions of Nahuatl, for instance, and to show what categories, what grammatical categories are working in Nahuatl, what the structure of that language is.

So I think this is really important, but we did not know this of Humboldt. The Nahuatl grammar was not published until 1994, and nobody knew Humboldt as a descriptive linguist.

JMc: So linguists in the nineteenth century were much more interested in this dead skeleton of the languages and took absolutely no interest in the character, and as you were saying yourself, Humboldt never really succeeded in developing his linguistics of character himself.

JT: Yes.

JMc: Why do you think that might be?

JT: There are also political reasons. German linguists, like Grimm and Bopp, were also reconstructing the past of the nation, and of Europe. The Grimms dealt with Germanic languages. I mean, they called their grammar *Deutsche Grammatik*, but it's a Germanic grammar. It's a comparative grammar of the Germanic languages, not at all a German grammar. And here comes Bopp, and what does he do? He compares the Indo-European languages. He does not go beyond, and he even tries to integrate non-Indo-European languages into the Indo-European family, like Polynesian, for instance. He writes against Humboldt. He actively wants to integrate the Austronesian languages into the Indo-European family, and Humboldt was trying to show just the contrary. So I think Germany, Europe were the aim, the final aim of historical linguistics. And the other guys who dealt with non-Indo-European languages, they were the minority. They were mostly Orientalists, Sinologists, and so on dealing with oriental languages, Chinese, Egyptian, but they were not at the very centre of linguistics.

JMc: But a figure like Schleicher, for example, was at the very centre mid-nineteenth-century, and of course Schleicher developed his theory of morphology, which is essentially a kind of typology from a present-day perspective and does have pretensions to accounting for the structure of all languages.

JT: Yes, of course, but here, I would say, we do not have the European or German theme any more; here we have the scientific theme, so we have Darwinism, and of course the influence of natural sciences is very strong here. Hence we have to create, like Darwin did for the species, a tree for the development of all languages of mankind. Yes, that is true, but morphology was always at the very centre. I mean, morphology, this is what what Schlegel, Friedrich Schlegel, discovered when he said we have to look at the *Struktur*. He uses the term *Struktur*, *innere Struktur*, for the first time, and we have to look at the *Struktur* and not at the vocabulary for the comparison of languages. And this is what Bopp does immediately when he writes a *Conjugationssystem*. It's on *Konjugation*. It's not on semantics. It does not compare, as Peter Simon Pallas for instance did, words, lexicon, as the basis of his comparative approach, but he then already goes into *Konjugation*, and then, of course, the Grimms go into *Deutsche Grammatik*. First, they write the *Deutsche Grammatik* before they go on to the *Wörterbuch*. And then, of course, after the Grimms, everybody in Europe writes comparative grammars – grammar of the Romance languages, grammar of the Slavic languages, and so on and so forth – so this becomes a huge success. After the Grimms, Bopp and then all the others do comparative grammars, and hence the focus is on morphology, and morphology means also they're not dealing so very much with the meaning of those morphemes, but they're more with the form, with the material form of morphemes.

JMc: Yes, that's very true. I mean, Schleicher says himself that he can't penetrate into the inner form of languages. He just sticks to the surface. So this brings us to the last question, which is about Humboldt's term "inner form". This is probably one of the most iconic Humboldtian terms, "inner form", but Humboldt used the term only in passing himself, and later scholars, right up to the twentieth century, have used it in myriad different senses. So why do you think this term has captured people's imaginations in the way that it has, and what do you think the significance of the term was for Humboldt himself?

JT: Let's start with the first part. "Inner form" comes up in the *Kawi-Einleitung*. After writing some chapters on external form, *äußere Form*, or the *Lautform*, Humboldt writes a chapter on inner form, *innere Sprachform*. What is *innere Sprachform*? What does Humboldt talk about in this chapter? He talks about the semantics of words, and he talks about the semantics of grammatical categories, so this is *innere Form*. *Innere Form* just means the meaning, and then he goes on and talks about the conjunction of meaning and sound. So the next chapter after the chapter on *innere Sprachform* is about both meaning and sound going together. So, and I think the term *innere Sprachform* has been exaggerated by the readers of Humboldt, certainly, but I think they saw something really correct in the end, because this is the very centre of his thought. If we go back to my answer to your first question, I think that going into semantics and into the meaning of categories of morphemes, this is the inner form.

And this is really what is the very centre of Humboldt's dealing with languages, because he wants to show *la merveilleuse variété des opérations de notre esprit*, the marvellous variety of the operations of our mind. And mind is the inner form, so even if the chapter on inner form is very short, the readers of Humboldt were correct in focusing on this term, because this is the very novelty of his approach: to look not only at the variety of the sounds. That languages have different sounds was clear from Aristotle onwards, and this material diversity was clear from antiquity on. But Bacon, Locke, Leibniz, and Herder, Humboldt, they see: no, it's not only sound that differs in languages. It's the meaning. It's the mind. It's the inner form, and I think therefore the focus on inner form is really justified.

JMc: OK, although I guess meaning and semantics, those are potentially anachronistic terms, because if you think of how semantics is done today – like truth-functional semantics, for example – there's an idea that meaning is something objective, but for Humboldt inner form is perhaps something much more mystical, talking about the operations of the mind.

JT: No, not so much. No, because for instance, in his first discourse at the Academy, where he tries to find an answer, why we have to do linguistics, he proposes that we now have to describe all the languages of the world. We have to do *vergleichendes Sprachstudium*, descriptive-comparative, descriptive *Linguistik*.

JMc: OK.

JT: And then Humboldt asks, why do we do comparative linguistics, and then at the end, he talks about the semantics of words, quite clearly. He says that words that refer to feelings, to interior operations of the mind, differ more from language to language. Words for exterior objects, they differ less. However, they still differ. A sheep might be something different in, let's say, in Nahuatl and in French and so on. So I think there is this focus on the meaning, which he calls *Begriff*, by the way. He does not talk about *Bedeutung*. His term is *Begriff*, and the *Begriff* here can be different in different languages.

JMc: So you might call *Begriff* "concept" in English, do you think?

JT: Yes, I would say concept. But *Begriff* or concept, after Hegel and rationalism, was too closely aligned with the mind. A better word is perhaps *Vorstellung*, because it's less rationalistic, because this is exactly what the mind does. The mind does create *Vorstellungen* – this is how Humboldt describes it: the world goes through the senses into the mind, and the mind then creates *Vorstellungen*. And they are immediately connected to sound, so they're immediately words.

JMc: So in English we might say "representation" or "image" for *Vorstellung*, do you think?

JT: Why not?

JMc: Yeah. Why not?

JT: "Image" is also not bad because the word, as Humboldt says, is something between image and sign. Sign is the completely arbitrary thing with the universal concept. Image is something concrete, which depicts the world, and the word is something in between. It has a special structure, a special position between sign and image. Sometimes the word can be an *Abbild*, an image, and sometimes it can also be used as a sign, but this is possible because it is in between the sign and the image. And perhaps one word on this problem: right in the chapter on the *innere Form*, he adds that we might compare the word, or the work of the mind creating a language, with the work of an artist. So that is exactly what he is thinking. He says that languages work like artists, you see: they create images.

JMc: OK. Excellent. Well, thank you very much for this conversation.

JT: Thank you very much for the interesting questions.

Primary sources

Bopp, Franz. 1816. *Über das Conjugationssystem der Sanskritsprache in Vergleichung mit jenem der griechischen, lateinischen, persischen und germanischen Sprache.* Frankfurt am Main: Andräische Buchhandlung.

Bopp, Franz. 1820. Analytical comparison of the Sanskrit, Greek, Latin, and Teutonic languages, shewing the original identity of their grammatical structure. *Annals of Oriental Literature* (1). 1–64.

Bopp, Franz. 1845–1853. *A comparative grammar of the Sanskrit, Zend, Greek, Latin, Lithuanian, Gothic, German, and Sclavonic languages.* Trans. by Edward B. Eastwick. 3 vols. London: Madden & Malcolm.

Bopp, Franz. 1857–1861. *Vergleichende Grammatik des Sanskrit, Send, Armenischen, Griechischen, Lateinischen, Litauischen, Altslavischen, Gothischen und Deutschen.* 2nd ed. 3 vols. Berlin: Dümmler.

Grimm, Jacob. 1819. *Deutsche Grammatik.* Göttingen: Dieterich'sche Buchhandlung.

Grimm, Jacob. 1822–1837. *Deutsche Grammatik.* 4 vols. Göttingen: Dieterich'sche Buchhandlung.

Grimm, Jacob & Wilhelm et al. Grimm. 1854–1960. *Deutsches Wörterbuch.* 16 vols. Leipzig: Hirzel.

Humboldt, Wilhelm von. 1836. *Über die Verschiedenheit des menschlichen Sprachbaues: Über die Kawi-Sprache auf der Insel Java.* Alexander von Humboldt (ed.). Berlin: Dümmler.

Humboldt, Wilhelm von. 1988 [1836]. *On language. The diversity of human language structure and its influence on the mental development of mankind.* Trans. by Peter Heath. Cambridge: Cambridge University Press.

Humboldt, Wilhelm von. 1994. *Mexikanische Grammatik.* Manfred Ringmacher (ed.). Paderborn: Schöningh.

Humboldt, Wilhelm von. 1997. *Essays on language.* Trans. by Theo Harden & Daniel J. Farrelly. Frankfurt am Main: Lang.

Humboldt, Wilhelm von. 2012. *Baskische Wortstudien und Grammatik.* Bernhard Hurch (ed.). Paderborn: Schöningh.

Schlegel, Friedrich. 1808. *Ueber die Sprache und Weisheit der Indier.* Heidelberg: Mohr und Zimmer.

Schlegel, Friedrich. 1900 [1808]. On the Indian language, literature and philosophy. In E. J. Millington (ed.), *The æsthetic and miscellaneous works of Friedrich von Schlegel*, 425–536. London: George Bell.

Schleicher, August. 1850. *Die Sprachen Europas in systematischer Übersicht.* Bonn: König.

Schleicher, August. 1863. *Die Darwinische Theorie und die Sprachwissenschaft, offenes Sendschreiben an Herrn Dr. Ernst Haeckel, o. Professor der Zoologie und Direktor des zoologischen Museums an der Universität Jena.* Weimar: Hermann Böhlau.

Schleicher, August. 1869. *Darwinism tested by the science of language.* Trans. by Alex V. W. Bikkers. London: John Camden Hotton.

Vossler, Karl. 1904. *Positivismus und Idealismus in der Sprachwissenschaft.* Heidelberg: Winter.

Secondary sources

Aarsleff, Hans & John L. Logan. 2016. An essay on the context and formation of Wilhelm von Humboldt's linguistic thought. *History of European Ideas* 42(6). 729–807.

McElvenny, James. 2016. The fate of form in the Humboldtian tradition: the Formungstrieb of Georg von der Gabelentz. *Language and Communication* 47. 30–42.

McElvenny, James. 2018. August Schleicher and materialism in nineteenth-century linguistics. *Historiographia Linguistica* 45(1). 133–152.

Mueller-Vollmer, Kurt & Markus Messling. 2017. Wilhelm von Humboldt. In Edward N. Zalta (ed.), *The Stanford encyclopedia of philosophy.* https://plato.stanford.edu/archives/spr2017/entries/wilhelm-humboldt/.

Ringmacher, Manfred. 1996. *Organismus der Sprachidee: H. Steinthals Weg von Humboldt zu Humboldt.* Paderborn: Schöningh.

Trabant, Jürgen. 1986. *Apeliotes oder der Sinn der Sprache, Wilhelm von Humboldts Sprachbild.* München: Wilhelm Fink.

Trabant, Jürgen. 1992. *Humboldt ou le sens du langage.* With François Mortier and Jean-Luc Evard. Liège: Mardaga.

Trabant, Jürgen. 2012. *Weltansichten: Wilhelm von Humboldts Sprachprojekt.* München: C.H. Beck.

Trabant, Jürgen. 2015. *Wilhelm von Humboldt Lectures, Université de Rouen.* https://webtv.univ-rouen.fr/channels/#2015-wilhelm-von-humboldt-lectures.

Trabant, Jürgen. 2020. Science of language: India vs America: The science of language in 19th-century Germany. In Efraim Podoksik (ed.), *Doing humanities in nineteenth-century Germany*, 189–213. Leiden: Brill.

Chapter 2

Missionary grammars in Australia

Clara Stockigt[a] & James McElvenny[b]
[a]University of Adelaide [b]University of Siegen

JMc: As we saw in the previous interview with Jürgen Trabant, a key issue animating much European language scholarship in the nineteenth century was capturing and accounting for the diverse forms found in the world's languages. In this interview, we take a peek at some of the sources from which European scholars derived their knowledge of non-Indo-European languages. To introduce us to this topic, we're joined by Clara Stockigt from the University of Adelaide, who's a specialist in the history of language documentation in Australia.

Before we get started, we have to note that our discussion today focuses rather narrowly on the technical details of the grammatical description of Australian languages and the intellectual networks within which the authors of early grammars operated. We therefore miss the broader – and in many ways much more important – story of settler colonialism in Australia and the world more generally and how this was intertwined with scientific research. This is a topic that we address elsewhere in the podcast series.

So Clara, to put us in the picture, could you tell us which languages were the first to be described in detail in Australia?

CS: The languages that were described initially were those spoken around the colonial capitals. You had, for example, missionary Lancelot Threlkeld writing a grammar of the language spoken near Newcastle, which is reasonably close to Sydney. The languages spoken close to Adelaide on the coast were described by Lutheran missionaries in the 1840s. Charles Symmons, who was the Protector of Aborigines in Western Australia, described the language spoken close to Perth,

 Clara Stockigt & James McElvenny. 2022. Missionary grammars in Australia. In James McElvenny (ed.), *Interviews in the history of linguistics: Volume I*, 13–28. Berlin: Language Science Press. DOI: 10.5281/zenodo.7096290

so in the very early era you have a pattern where the languages spoken close to the colonial capitals were described.

But those first missions didn't last very long, and the languages, the people, dispersed quite quickly. Subsequently the Lutherans established missions in South Australia among the Diyari and the Arrernte, and at those missions, there was this intergenerational tradition of linguistic description where Aboriginal people and the missionaries worked alongside each other in what was an economic unit.

JMc: So did the languages that were described in these centres all belong to a single family? How many language families are there in Australia?

CS: We have the Pama-Nyungan family, which covers most of the Australian continent, and so all of the languages that we're talking about, having been grammatically described in the nineteenth century, belonged to this Pama-Nyungan family of languages, which is a higher-order overarching umbrella under which different languages belong. About 250 Pama-Nyungan languages are said to have been spoken in Australia at the time of colonization.

JMc: And so what was the motivation of the missionaries to study these languages in Australia?

CS: As everywhere around the world Australian missionaries described languages in order to preach in the local language and convert people to Christianity. They believed that if people could hear the Gospel in their mother tongue, they would necessarily be converted to Christianity. The Lutheran missionaries in Central Australia prepared and had printed vernacular literacy materials in Diyari and in Arrernte. As Aboriginal people became literate in their own language, they were able to use hymn books and books of prayer in the schools and in church services. It's also clear that many missionaries wanted to describe the complexity of the languages in order to show that the people speaking the language were intelligent. From their point of view, you couldn't covert a people to Christianity unless they were intelligent, and by laying out the complexity of the language, they were, in a way, demonstrating the promise of their mission work. Missionary grammarians in Australia also realized that their work was going to preserve the languages that they were describing. You know, there was a perception that Australian languages and Aboriginal people were disappearing very quickly in the aftermath of European settlement. Lancelot Threlkeld, who was Australia's earliest grammarian, who wrote a first complete grammar in 1834, he perceived that he had actually outlived the last speakers of the language he described in the 1820s and 1830s.

JMc: "Disappearing" sounds a bit passive and euphemistic. How did the missionaries, people like Threlkeld, describe the situation themselves?

CS: They used the word "disappearing".

JMc: OK.

CS: Yes. "Vanishing".

JMc: It seems a bit euphemistic, doesn't it? Do you think that that is how someone like Threlkeld genuinely felt about it, or do you think he was more interested in not offending his European readership?

CS: I think he perceived Australian populations were being decimated and dying out. And, of course, the nineteenth-century records collected by the missionaries are increasingly important today in reconstructing Australia's pre-invasion linguistic ecology because of the high rate of extinction of Australian Indigenous languages since colonization and also – or because – a large proportion of Australian Indigenous populations today now speak English, or Aboriginal English, or creoles as their first language.

JMc: And were missionaries just writing for other missionaries? Did they intend their grammars to be read only by other members of their missionary society?

CS: Some missionaries did, especially the ones who just wrote their grammars as German manuscripts, but those who knew that the work was going to be published often had a little section in the introduction saying that they hoped the work would be interesting, would be of value, to the interested philologist, so there was a definite sense that the missionaries were aware that their linguistic knowledge was valuable to readers outside the field. They were courting a relationship with European philologists.

JMc: What kind of experience did these missionaries have in grammar or in learning foreign languages which might have given them exposure to grammatical description of other languages?

CS: The missionaries who wrote grammars of Australian languages had received different degrees of linguistic training in preparation for mission work. Those trained at the Jänicke-Rückert schools, or at Neuendettelsau in Germany, or at the Basel Mission institute in Switzerland are said to have received a rigorous linguistic training with exposure to nineteenth-century grammars of Latin, Greek, and Hebrew.

JMc: Hebrew as well as Latin and Greek. Hebrew's a non-Indo-European language, of course, so structurally quite different from Latin and Greek.

CS: Yes.

JMc: So they would have been familiar with languages that have a structure not the same as their own native language?

CS: That's right, but only some of the grammarians had looked at Hebrew.

JMc: So it was a minority.

CS: Yes, I think so. On the other hand, other missionary grammarians, such as the Congregationalist George Taplin and Missionary Threlkeld of the London Mission Society, had received little formal training, and grammars written by the Protectors of Aborigines were founded in a well-rounded education and a knowledge of schoolboy Latin. So an assumption that a rigorously trained grammarian who had studied a greater number of classical languages would make better analyses of Australian linguistic structures than grammarians with lesser training is actually not upheld when we compare the quality of the description with what is known about a grammarian's training.

JMc: And why do you think that might be?

CS: Well, it's a bit odd. It might be because the sample size in Australia is reasonably small. But the fact that it appears to have little bearing on the quality of a grammatical description is probably because the strength of an individual description has more to do with the length of time and the type of exposure that a grammarian had with the language and probably also just to do with his inherent intelligence and aptitude.

JMc: OK. Although you'd think that you'd need to have some sort of grammatical framework that you could use as a scaffolding to even begin making your description.

CS: I think just a basic knowledge of Latin, a very basic knowledge of Latin, was enough to get you there.

JMc: Sort of bootstrapping.

CS: Yeah, and some missionary grammarians in Australia also had previous exposure to the structure of other exotic languages or non-European languages like Hebrew. Early Lutherans trained at the Jänicke-Rückert school were probably also aware of descriptions of Tamil because of missionary work in India.

JMc: OK, and Tamil is of course a Dravidian language, so another very different language, different kind of structure.

CS: Yes.

JMc: And I guess we should probably point out that we're using this term "exotic" a bit, but that's a category that the missionaries would have used themselves to describe these unfamiliar languages.

CS: Yeah. The missionaries in Australia tended to use the word "peculiar" rather than "exotic".

Missionary Threlkeld had worked in Polynesia, so he had some knowledge of the description of Polynesian languages from the mission field, and the Basel-trained missionary Handt had worked in Sierra Leone, so the way in which these experiences may have influenced the early description of Australian languages requires a lot more research, I think. Nobody's really looked into that too much.

JMc: OK, so this is an unexplored area of missionary linguistics.

CS: I think so, and especially the connection between the early description of languages in Polynesia and in Australia, because there were strong connections with missionaries from the London Missionary Society.

JMc: So how did these people writing grammars and word lists of Australian languages approach them, would you say?

CS: So as was the case with the description of other exotic languages–

JMc: Or peculiar languages, as the case may be.

CS: Or peculiar languages, yeah. Eurocentric linguistic understanding skewed the nineteenth-century representations of Australian linguistic structures. When we look at the attempts to represent the sound systems of Australian languages, we see that nineteenth-century linguists were presented with really significant challenges. Consonants in Australian languages typically show few articulatory manners and an absence of fricatives and affricates, but extensive places, extensive sets of place of articulation contrasts, some having two series of palatal and two series of apical phonemes for stops, nasals, and laterals. And it was difficult for European ears to distinguish these sounds, let alone to decide on a standardized way to represent them. So before the middle decades of the twentieth century, the orthographic treatments of Australian phonologies grossly underrepresented phonemic articulation contrasts, and all sources just fell well short of the mark. And I think it's this type of failure that has contributed to the outright dismissal of the early descriptions of Australian languages by some later twentieth-century researchers.

JMc: Even though the orthographies that early grammarians designed for these languages might have been insufficient, do you think that they still understood the principles of how the phonology of those languages worked, or do you think it just completely went past them?

CS: I think they understood that there was a greater level of complexity or there were things going on that they weren't grappling with, and they were frustrated with the inconsistencies in the system. So in the 1930s, when people started to look back at the earlier nineteenth-century sources, they could see that there was a great inconsistency, and even though early grammarians often aimed towards a uniform orthography and stated that they were following the conventions established by the Royal Geographical Society, they really just were not getting anywhere near an adequate method of representing the languages, and I don't think they understood what was going on, necessarily.

JMc: So those are the phonological features of the languages. What about in terms of the grammar?

CS: So missionary grammarians, by and large, opted to scaffold their developing understanding of Australian languages within the traditional European descriptive framework that they were familiar with from their study of classical languages. And as a consequence, missionary grammarians in Australia tended to attempt to describe features that were just not present in Australian languages, including indefinite and definite articles, the comparative marking of adjectives, passive constructions, and relative clauses signalled by relative pronouns.

JMc: So do you think that the missionaries were actually implying that those categories were universals and were projecting them into the languages they were describing, or do you think it was intended more as a heuristic, as a learner's guide, like they were writing for an audience that might want to express the equivalent of a passive construction in their own language in this Australian language, and so the grammar is saying, "If you had this kind of structure in a European language, you would then use this"?

CS: That's exactly what they were doing. So on the other hand, grammarians who became reasonably familiar with an Australian language encountered an array of foreign – or, as they called them, "peculiar" – morphosyntactic features that were not originally accommodated within the descriptive model, and they invented new terminology and descriptive solutions in order to describe these peculiarities. And so they were able to account for Australian features like the marking and function of ergative case, the large morphological case systems of Australian languages, sensitivity of case marking to animacy, systems of bound pronouns, inalienably possessed noun phrases, inclusive and exclusive pronominal distinction and the morphological marking of clause subordination. All of these features were described in the earliest era in Australia. And some early Australian grammarians were certainly aware that the traditional grammatical framework was inadequate to properly describe Australian structures. In 1844, for instance, Lutheran missionary Schürmann advised that grammarians of Australian languages should "divest their mind as much as possible of preconceived ideas, particularly of those grammatical forms which they may have acquired by the study of ancient or modern languages."

JMc: Wow, so that's a direct quote from Schürmann..

CS: Yeah, and that's 1844, so a reasonably early perception, I think. But nevertheless, these missionary grammarians appear unwilling to wean themselves off the framework designed to accommodate classical European languages, even when they knew that the framework was less than adequate. And this is probably because the traditional framework conveyed peculiar structures in a way that was most accessible and easy for the reader to understand, as you were suggesting earlier.

So these grammarians who perceived that the framework was inadequate still managed to describe foreign linguistic structures by subverting the traditional framework. Section or chapter headings that are built into the traditional framework that accommodated European structures that are not found in Australian languages sometimes provided a useful, vacant slot into which these newly encountered peculiarities could be inserted into the description. So an example here, just to get a bit technical, is the description of the case suffix marking allative function, which tended to be underrepresented in the early grammars because allative function is not marked by the morphological case systems of European languages.

JMc: OK, so allative is like going to a place.

CS: Yeah, that's right. But there was a group of grammarians in Australia who exemplified allative case marking under the heading "correlative pronouns", which is an unnecessary descriptive category when it's applied to Australian languages. So under this heading, "correlative pronouns", we see noun phrases translated as "from X in ablative case" and "to X in allative case", but there's no suggestion that the morphology that was described under this heading, "correlative pronouns", was in any way pronominal. And similarly, while grammarians happily accommodated the large morphological case systems of Australian languages within an early chapter of the grammar headed "Nouns" by presenting case paradigms of up to 11 cases, these same grammarians presented the same morphology again in a later section of the grammar under a final chapter headed "Prepositions". A contradiction in describing suffixing affixes under the word class heading "preposition" doesn't appear to have perturbed the grammarian. Newly encountered Australian features tended to be accounted for in sections of the grammar that conventionally conveyed a Europeanism that was perceived as functionally equivalent to the Australian feature – in this instance, nouns marked for cases that needed to be translated by an English prepositional phrase being described as a preposition. And other instances of this type of substitution process in which the traditional framework was colonized by foreign structures include the construal of ergative morphology as marking passive constructions, the depiction of bound or enclitic pronouns as verbal inflections for number and person, and the description of deictic forms as third-person neuter pronouns.

JMc: And how widespread is this representation of ergative morphology as a kind of passive construction? How many different scholars do that?

CS: Quite a few. Even though they made a good account of ergative morphology when they're talking about case, either conceiving of the ergative case as a second nominative or a type of ablative case, but often when it comes to the description of the passive or the part of the grammar where you're expected to describe passive functions, there will be ergative morphology given there as well.

JMc: What connections were there between the people in the field writing descriptions of Australian languages and linguistic scholars in Europe and other parts of the world? Were there active networks of communication between the field and the metropolitan centres, and did these language descriptions feed back into the development of linguistic theory?

CS: Generally not. I think connections between missionary grammarians in Australia and Europe were quite limited. Australian linguistic material tends to be absent from nineteenth-century comparative philological literature, and European philologists commonly mention a scarcity, or they're frustrated about a scarcity, of Australian linguistic data. There's no reference to Australian languages in Pott (1974 [1884–1890]), nor in Friedrich Max Müller (1864), although there is a reasonably comprehensive discussion of Australian material in the final volume of Prichard's *Physical History of Mankind*, Volume 5, 1847.

JMc: OK, and that's quite early, 1847.

CS: Yeah.

JMc: So what material did he have to work with?

CS: He had the grammars that had been published at that stage, which were from South Australia and New South Wales, so there was a relatively small amount of material, but he had looked at what was available at that time, which makes it odd that these later compilations of linguistic material from around the world don't reference the Australian material.

JMc: So were these Australian grammars published, or were they manuscripts?

CS: The ones that he referred to were published grammars. There was a wave of publications of materials in the 1830s and 1840s, and then not a lot of published material until towards the end of that century.

JMc: And were they published in Australia or in Europe?

CS: They were published in Australia, generally by colonial authorities.

JMc: The missionary grammarians themselves, was there contact between them, out in the field, or did they work alone mostly?

CS: They pretty much worked alone, not only from developments in Europe, but also in intellectual isolation from each other. Many early grammarians appear to have written their grammars without any knowledge of previous descriptions of Australian languages. Where schools of Australian linguistic thought did develop or where ideas about the best way to describe Australian languages were handed down to future grammarians, you see a regional pattern of ideas about the best way to describe Australian languages developing. And this occurred within different Christian denominations which were ethnically and linguistically distinct and which had their headquarters in different pre-Federation Australian colonial capitals.

JMc: And what were the main regions?

CS: So we had a school of description developing in New South Wales – the earliest grammars of Australian languages were written there – and then the school of description developing in South Australia mostly with the Lutheran missionaries, and then a later descriptive school developing in Queensland. So this decentralized nature of the development of linguistics in Australia hampered improvements to the understandings and descriptive practices in the country, but also to the movement of ideas in and out of the country. But just as some of the early grammarians had flirted with the interested philologist in the introductory passages, the linguistic knowledge of some grammarians was actively sought by some scholars outside the country. The pathways through which ideas about Australian languages were exchanged remain largely untraced, although there has been focused interest on the enduring communication between the Lutheran missionary Carl Strehlow, who worked with the Arrernte populations in Central Australia, and his German editor, Moritz von Leonhardi. And this relationship kept Strehlow abreast of early twentieth-century European ethnological thinking, although linguistics played a relatively small part in their intellectual exchange.

JMc: When was Carl Strehlow working?

CS: He was working with the Arrernte from 1894 until his death in 1922.

JMc: OK, so this is right at the end of the nineteenth century.

CS: Yeah, in the beginning of the twentieth century. But other interactions deserve more scholarly attention, including the interaction between Wilhelm Bleek, who was the German philologist based in South Africa and who, in 1858–1859, catalogued Sir George Grey's philological library, and missionary George Taplin, who was in South Australia, and himself collated comparative lexical material of South Australian languages. There's an interesting exchange between these two people that I think would be worthy of further investigation.

JMc: And of course, George Grey was a sort of wandering colonial official, wasn't he, so he had previously been in South Australia before he went to South Africa.

CS: Yeah. And in New Zealand as well. It was George Grey who supported the work of the Lutheran missionaries in South Australia in those very early years.

CS: Other lesser-known exchanges between Australia and Europe are Hans Co-nan von der Gabelentz's and Friedrich Müller's reframing of Australian erga-tive structures as passive, which were both based on a grammar written by the Lutheran missionary Meyer in 1843. These were given in Gabelentz's *Über das Passivum* in 1861 and Müller's *Grundriß der Sprachwissenschaft* in 1882.

JMc: Do you think that that is a fair interpretation of Hans Conan von der Gabe-lentz? Because I guess his *Über das Passivum* is really an early typological work, and he's talking essentially about a functional category and looking at how it is realized in what we would now call the different voice systems of languages around the world. So he doesn't just have Australian languages in there, for ex-ample. He also has Tagalog and numerous other diverse languages of the world. So do you think it's fair to say that he was reframing the ergative as a passive, or rather, he just used "passive" as a sort of typological term to describe this kind of voice structure in the languages of the world?

CS: No, I actually do think he reframed the structure and he reinterpreted the material that Meyer had presented in a way that Meyer had not intended, and I don't think it's a fair representation of the structure in an Australian language in order to support his theory.

JMc: OK. And how representative was the situation in Australia in comparison with other places that were subject to European colonialism in this period? So especially settler colonialism. The comparison, I guess, would be with South and especially North America and South Africa, and parts of the Pacific, like New Zealand.

CS: I think there's a lot more work to be done in comparing what occurred in these different areas, but I think the situation in Australia does differ quite a lot. No nineteenth-century descriptive linguist in Australia managed to truly bridge the divide between being a missionary or field-based linguist and academia, so Australia has no scholars equivalent to Franz Boas in North America or Wilhelm Bleek in South Africa. Channels of communication between Europe and Aus-tralia were much less developed than between Europe and other colonies.

JMc: Why is that? Just because it's so far away?

CS: Possibly because it's so far away, and I think because linguistics as a discipline wasn't centralized, and we just didn't happen to have a Wilhelm Bleek here or a Franz Boas. There wasn't a centralized development of ideas in the country and we have this haphazard regional, ad hoc development of ideas in different mission fields that weren't really feeding into a central body that was communicating with Europe. And I think also the exchange of ideas was largely unidirectional flowing out of the country rather than into the country, so for instance, the presentation of sound systems of Australian languages in systematic diagrams that set out consonant inventories in tables, mapping place of articulation against manner of articulation, occur reasonably regularly and early in European publications commencing with Lepsius in 1855, who presented the phonology of Kaurna in such a sort of gridded system. Also, Friedrich Müller in 1867 did a similar thing, and later European works right up until the 1930s were representing Australian phonologies in this way, but such presentations appear not to have been read by any grammarian in Australia, or if they were read, they weren't understood and they weren't assimilated into Australian practice. The earliest reasonable graphic representation of consonants made by an Australian researcher didn't occur until Arthur Capell's 1956 work entitled *A New Approach to Australian Languages*. I think the slow speed with which phonological science entered Australia is illustrative of what could almost be seen as a linguistic vacuum in the country before about 1930.

JMc: Capell had a university position, didn't he? So I guess it's this academic influence that you're pointing to.

CS: He did, yes. The university connection commenced very early in the 1930s: you had the first dissertations on Australian Aboriginal languages being written within the Department of Classics at the University of Adelaide and within the Department of Anthropology at the University of Sydney, but it wasn't until a few decades later that you had linguistic researchers within academic institutions working on Australian languages.

JMc: OK. Up until now, I thought that Australian linguistics burst forth fully formed from the brow of Bob Dixon.

CS: Some would have us believe that.

JMc: OK, so thank you very much for telling us all about the situation in Australia with missionary linguistics.

CS: Absolute pleasure, James. Thanks for inviting me.

Primary sources

Bleek, Wilhelm H. I. 1858–1859. Australia. In *The library of His Excellency Sir George Grey, K.C.B., philology*. London: Trübner & Co.

Capell, Arthur. 1956. *A new approach to Australian languages*. Sydney: University of Sydney.

Flierl, J. 1880. Dieri Grammatik [Comparative grammar of Diyari and Wangkangurru]. Unpublished ms., Lutheran Archives, Adelaide, Box 22 Immanuel Synod–Bethesda Mission, 306.510.

Gabelentz, Hans Conan von der. 1861. Über das Passivum: Eine sprachvergleichende Abhandlung. *Abhandlungen der philologisch-historischen Classe der Königlich-Sächsischen Gesellschaft der Wissenschaften* 8. 449–546.

Grey, George. 1839. *Vocabulary of the dialects spoken by the Aboriginal races of South-Western Australia*. Reproduction published by T. and W. Bone, London, 1840. Perth: Self-published.

Grey, George. 1841. *Journals of two expeditions of discovery in North-West and Western Australia, during the years 1837, '38, and '39*. 2 vols. London: T. & W. Boone.

Grey, George. 1845. On the languages of Australia, being an extract from a dispatch from Captain G. Grey, Governor of South Australia, to Lord Stanley. *The Journal of the Royal Geographical Society of London* 15. 365–367. http://www.jstor.org/stable/1797917.

Kempe, F.A.H. 1891. A grammar and vocabulary of the language spoken by the Aborigines of the Macdonnell Ranges, South Australia. *Transactions of the Royal Society of South Australia* 14. 1–54.

Leonhardi, Moritz von. 1901. *Letter to C. Strehlow 10/09/1901 written in Germany*. Strehlow Research Centre, The NT Interpreter and Translator Service, 1901-1-2. Alice Springs.

Lepsius, Karl Richard. 1855. *Das allgemeine linguistische Alphabet: Grundsätze der Übertragung fremder Schriftsysteme und bisher noch ungeschriebener Sprachen in europäische Buchstaben*. Berlin: Wilhelm Hertz.

Lepsius, Karl Richard. 1863. *Standard alphabet for reducing unwritten languages and foreign graphic systems to a uniform orthography in European letters*. London: Williams & Norgate.

Meyer, Heinrich A. E. 1843. *Vocabulary of the language spoken by the Aborigines of the southern portions of the settled districts of South Australia, ... Preceded by a grammar*. Adelaide: James Allen.

Müller, Friedrich. 1867. *Reise der österreichischen Fregatte Novara um die Erde in den Jahren 1857, 1858, 1859: Linguistischer Theil, Abteilung III, australische Sprachen.* Vienna: Gerold's Sohn. 239–266.

Müller, Friedrich. 1882. *Grundriß der Sprachwissenschaft, Vol II: Die Sprachen der schlichthaarigen Rassen, Theil 1: Die Sprachen der australischen, der hyperboreischen und der amerikanischen Rasse.* Vienna: Hölder.

Müller, Friedrich Max. 1854. *Letters to Chevalier Bunsen on the classification of the Turanian languages.* London: A. & G. A. Spottiswoode.

Müller, Friedrich Max. 1864. *Lectures on the science of language delivered at the Royal Institution of Great Britain in February, March, April and May 1863: Second series.* See pages 103–175 for "The physiological alphabet". London: Longman.

Pott, August Friedrich. 1974 [1884–1890]. Einleitung in die allgemeine Sprachwissenschaft. In E. F. Konrad Koerner (ed.), *Einleitung in die Allgemeine Sprachwissenschaft* (1884–1890) together with *Zur Literatur der Sprachenkunde Europas* (Leipzig, 1887), 197–488. Philadelphia: Benjamins.

Prichard, James C. 1847. *Physical history of mankind.* Vol. V. London: Sherwood, Gilbert & Piper.

Royal Geographical Society. 1885. System of orthography for native names of places. *Proceedings of the Royal Geographical Society and Monthly Record of Geography* 7. 535–536.

Schürmann, Clamor W. 1844. *A vocabulary of the Parnkalla language spoken by the natives inhabiting the western shores of Spencer Gulf. To which is prefixed a collection of grammatical rules hitherto ascertained by C. W. Schürmann.* Adelaide: George Dahane.

Strehlow, Carl F. T. 1907–1920. *Die Aranda- und Loritja-Stämme in Zentral-Australien.* Vol. 1–5. Frankfurt am Main: Städtisches Völkerkunde-Museum.

Symmons, Charles. 1841. *Grammatical introduction to the study of the Aboriginal language in Western Australia.* Repr. in The Western Australian Almanac, Perth, 1842: *Grammar of the language spoken by the Aborigines of Western Australia.* Perth: Self-published.

Taplin, George. 1879. *The folklore, manners, customs, and languages of the South Australian Aborigines.* Adelaide: E. Spiller, Government Printer.

Threlkeld, Lancelot E. 1834. *An Australian grammar: Comprehending the principles and natural rules of the language, as spoken by the Aborigines in the vicinity of Hunter's River, Lake Macquarie, etc., New South Wales.* Sydney: Stephens & Stokes.

Secondary sources

Dixon, Robert M. W. 2010. *The languages of Australia.* Cambridge: Cambridge University Press.

Simpson, Jane. 2019. Why women botanists outnumbered women linguists in nineteenth century Australia. *History and Philosophy of the Language Sciences.* https://hiphilangsci.net/2019/05/01/women-botanists-women-linguists/.

Stockigt, Clara. 2015. Early descriptions of Pama-Nyungan Ergativity. *Historiographia Linguistica* 42(2–3). 335–377.

Stockigt, Clara. 2017. *Pama-nyungan morphosyntax: Lineages of early description.* University of Adelaide. (doctoral thesis.). DOI: 10.4225/55/5926388950cdc.

Stockigt, Clara. Forthcoming. *Australian Pama-Nyungan languages: lineages of early description.* Berlin: Language Science Press.

Chapter 3

Disciplinary linguistics in the nineteenth century

Floris Solleveld[a] & James McElvenny[b]

[a]University of Leuven [b]University of Siegen

JMc: In this interview, we're joined by Floris Solleveld from the University of Leuven, who's going to give us an overview of how linguistics emerged as a discipline in the nineteenth century.

So Floris, what was the character of language scholarship and the humanities more generally in the nineteenth century? We have already talked a little bit in this podcast about how nineteenth-century language scholars emphasized the novelty of what they were doing, that there were frequent proclamations of a revolution in the language sciences. You've examined this question yourself in quite a bit of detail. Do you think that there was a decisive break in the study of language and the human world in the nineteenth century, and could it be described as a scientific revolution?

FS: Hi, James. Thanks for having me here. Well, the question to what extent you can speak of a scientific revolution in the humanities is a question that I have pondered for some six years, and my general, unspectacular answer is: Kind of. A lot of things happened, a lot of things changed, around 1800. There is a lot of revolutionary rhetoric surrounding these changes, and whether you call it a scientific revolution depends on your theoretical perspective and on your personal preferences.

But what happens in linguistics actually is quite dramatic. What you see is a breaking of paper trails, which is a good indication that something drastic is

Floris Solleveld & James McElvenny. 2022. Disciplinary linguistics in the nineteenth century. In James McElvenny (ed.), *Interviews in the history of linguistics: Volume I*, 29–39. Berlin: Language Science Press. DOI: 10.5281/zenodo.7096292

happening, if people stop using work from a previous period, stop quoting from it. And that is what happens in nineteenth-century linguistics. They're not using eighteenth-century work much any more, and there is a staple of revolutionary rhetoric surrounding it.

Friedrich Schlegel is the outstanding example. The man is a serial proclaimer of revolutions. Even as a student, he proclaims a revolution in the study of antiquity. Then he invents the Romantic movement, and then he proclaims an Oriental renaissance in his *Ueber die Sprache und Weisheit der Indier*. And most of his proclamations get picked up, although not exactly in the way that he intended them. That is, he is not the guy who founds modern classical philology. His Oriental renaissance turns out to become the basis of comparative linguistics rather than the basis of a spiritual rejuvenation of the West, but to get that instead is not a crass failure either.

And if you look at that rhetoric in retrospect, which is what happens in the nineteenth century as the discipline develops, you see that people actually look back on it in those terms, as a revolution.

But there is a bit of a grey area. For instance, the first person to actually speak of a scientific revolution in the study of language is Peter Stephen Du Ponceau. And what does he cite as an example? He doesn't cite Schlegel. He cites Adelung, *Mithridates*, which is the text that people now typically use to contrast the previous paradigm and new historical-comparative linguistics. But then Adelung was still used as a source of data, and that is remarkable: Adelung is basically the only or one of the few that are still used as a source of information after the beginning of the century.

JMc: Do you think even though there are all of these proclamations of revolutions and people are not citing their predecessors that this really represents a break in continuity between the way people were doing the study of language in the nineteenth century and their predecessors and also a break in the way that they thought about language, the philosophy of language and the philosophy of science that lies behind the discipline of linguistics?

FS: Yes, I do think so, and not just in having this historical-comparative perspective, which of course is very pre-eminent in nineteenth-century linguistics. There is also a break, for instance, in the realization that there are these different language families, each with their own character, or with the idea that you can actually analyse language structures in different ways, because these different language families have different organizational principles. And that is reflected in the way linguistic material is used, in the mapping of sound systems or the analysis of different ways of ordering particles. You already see Humboldt splitting up Polynesian languages morphologically in *Über die Kawi-Sprache.* You already see Richard Lepsius drawing up diagrams of sound systems in the presentation of his phonetic alphabet, and that is the sort of analysis of language which really doesn't happen in the eighteenth century. So yes, I do think that there is this drastic discontinuity.

You also see that the term "linguistics" comes up in this period. Actually, the remarkable thing again is that the first people to use the term "linguistics" are late eighteenth-century German compilers who very much work within an early modern compilatory style, so in that regard you never really have a clean break. But then scientific revolutions aren't like political revolutions where you storm the Bastille or the Winter Palace, you chop off the king's head and you say it's a revolution and nobody doubts it.

With scientific revolutions, you always have this sort of unclarity about what the measure of a complete conceptual break should be. And this is one reason why there has been a lot of scepticism about the notion of scientific revolutions in the history of science, and why some people want to get rid of the phrase. Lorraine Daston and Katherine Park talked about getting rid of that "ringing three-word phrase." Steven Shapin said, "There was no such thing as the Scientific Revolution, and this is a book about it."

And that sort of sums up the *communis opinio* among historians of science. But in the history of scholarship, the question has been addressed far less. Within the humanities, I think the history of linguistics stands out for this sort of really radical conceptual break and break in ways in which material is organized and knowledge is being produced. For the humanities at large, my answer is more like "kind of", maybe a qualified yes, but linguistics really is one of the strongest arguments in favour of that.

JMc: So would you say that accompanying the scientific revolution in linguistics there was a fundamental change in the sociological constitution of the field, and in scholarship more generally, in the nineteenth century? To describe the scholarly community up until the end of the eighteenth century, it's usual to talk about the Republic of Letters. Do you think that this was superseded in the nineteenth century by clear-cut university-based disciplines, or do you think that there was continuity from this earlier idea of the Republic of Letters?

FS: The Republic of Letters is a container notion for the learned world, which perceives itself as an independent commonwealth, hence republic, *res publica,* of letters. And "letters" here is an early modern term for learning at large; "letters" really means what it means in the name-shield of the Faculty of Letters. And three things actually hold that community together, which is (a) a correspondence network reinforced by learned journalism, (b) a symbolic economy, and (c) the sense of an academic community. Now, these things, these three aspects, they actually persist. We still perceive ourselves as part of an imagined community. We still correspond with each other. We still trade in information and prestige, and we don't get rich, generally. So to that extent, that sort of infrastructure persists.

Still the notion of Republic of Letters pretty much fades out from use in the early nineteenth century. I've traced that, and it is pretty much a sad story of decline. Some people try to reinvent it – doesn't work. And there are very clear explanations for that. First of all, the notion of "republic" is appropriated by the French Revolution, and gets different connotations. The notion of "letters" changes, or "literature" becomes a term for literature as an art form instead for learning at large. We still speak of the literature in our field, and that is sort of a remnant of that early modern use. And also, people now address their peers, or they address a wider public, or in some cases they address the nation, and they don't address the learned community in that sense anymore.

So it didn't make that much sense for nineteenth-century scholars to appeal to the Republic of Letters any more. As it did make sense, for instance, for late seventeenth-century Huguenot journalists who reinvented the notion, and it did make sense for the *parti philosophique*, who appropriated – or rather, violently took over – the Republic of Letters in the mid-eighteenth century. It made sense also for German academics who were trying to position themselves in the eighteenth century.

But this idea of an amateur community being superseded by professionalism, that story has to be seriously qualified, because scholarship already is concentrated at universities in the German lands in the late seventeenth and eighteenth century. That is actually what gives the German-speaking countries an edge in the nineteenth century, because then it turns out that universities are a much more effective model for concentrating learning than they seem to be in the late early modern period, whereas what happens in the French- and English-speaking world is that this concentration of scholarship at universities goes a lot slower.

It's actually only in the second half of the nineteenth century, and especially after 1870, that this model really becomes so predominant that amateur or independent scholarship becomes the great exception. 1870, of course, in France, means the end of the Second Empire because they lose the Franco-Prussian War, and then the Second Empire becomes the Third Republic. In Britain, from the 1860s onward, there is a huge wave of new university foundations, so-called red brick universities, and that really leads to a change in the academic landscape. There had been new university foundations before, King's College, University College London, Durham University, but those were more like additions to the Oxbridge duopoly and the Scottish big four or big five.

What happens with red brick universities is an intensification of academic research. If you look at the number of university staff and students in Europe from 1700 to 1850, it's pretty constant. There are some serious interruptions when the Jesuit Order is banished or when the French Revolution closes all the universities or when half the German universities die in the period between 1795 and 1818, but on the whole, the numbers are pretty constant. From the second half of the nineteenth century onward, it expands exponentially. So yes, the notion of Republic of Letters goes out of use in the early nineteenth century, but no, it's not as if there is this clean break from an amateur learned community to institutional professional scholarship within well-delineated disciplines.

But I do want to add a footnote to that, because Ian McNeely recently wrote an article about Humboldt's *Über die Kawi-Sprache* as the last project of the Republic of Letters. He says that Humboldt then pieced his information together from all kind of previous language gathering exercises like Adelung, like Hervás y Panduro, like the British colonial administrators in Southeast Asia, particularly Marsden, who then fed all that information into Humboldt's coffers - and then Humboldt, as a retired statesman and independent scholar, writes this big compendium which really still radiates the ghost of this imagined learned community. That is not untrue, but again, this is McNeely's schematism: he thinks of the Republic of Letters as a sort of reified scholarly community rather than as a notion that you use strategically to present your own situation.

If you look at how the languages of the world are mapped throughout the long nineteenth century, then quite a lot of these people actually are not university-based scholars. There is a process of institutionalization around historical-comparative linguistics. A small part of that is about linguistics proper and about Sanskrit, but a much larger part is about German studies, French studies, *Germanistik* and *Romanistik*, Slavonic studies a bit later, English studies, which are then informed by Indo-European comparative linguistics. But if you look at people who mapped the languages of India, the languages of Australia, the languages of Oceania, or the languages of the Americas, those are to a large part colonial administrators or people co-ordinating missionary networks. And those people do not operate any more within what they would describe as a Republic of Letters. George Grey in Cape Town and Auckland did not think of himself as a citizen of the Republic of Letters. George Grierson mapping the languages of India did not think of himself as a citizen of the Republic of Letters. Well, maybe Peter

Stephen Du Ponceau in Philadelphia – who, after all, was born in the eighteenth century and who still basically thrives on this correspondence network – maybe he thought of himself as a citizen of the Republic of Letters.

JMc: But how did they think of themselves, and how were they seen by the newly emerging caste of professional linguists in universities? Was their work received in the centre of disciplinary linguistics, in Indo-European comparative linguistics? Did it feed into that, or were they just doing something separate that was still considered to be an amateur project?

FS: Well, no, what you see is that they do take on board professional expertise. George Grey, again, is the outstanding example, for what does he do when he becomes Governor of South Africa and sets forth his language-gathering project which he already had been doing in Adelaide and Auckland? He hires Wilhelm Bleek, a German philologist with a PhD – actually the first student to get his PhD on African languages – to organize his library and to put a stamp of scientific approval on what George Grey had been doing.

You also see it with George Grierson, who writes – or co-ordinates – *The linguistic survey of India* and who tries to avoid acquiring a strong institutional foothold – although he has affiliations – so as to retain some sort of independence. He hires an assistant, Sten Konow, who is university-based. He gets honorary doctorates, he goes to Orientalist congresses.

Several of these people mapping the languages of the world get the Prix Volney. Peter Stephen Du Ponceau wins the Prix Volney. Sigismund Koelle wins the Prix Volney. Richard Lepsius, who later becomes a professor of Egyptology, gets the Prix Volney. So there is this sort of interaction between this broader ethnolinguistic project and the narrower discipline formation within linguistics, and you also see that some tools, especially phonetic alphabets, get developed within this broader network rather than within this narrow academic sphere.

Indo-European historical-comparative linguistics is predominant because they have institutional firepower. If you look at who holds the chairs in Germany – where indeed there are chairs in these fields much earlier on – it's largely Sanskritists and Germanists. And if you look at the number of people who are actually engaged in this mapping of the languages of the world, the number of people involved in a secondary sense that they supply information for it runs in thousands, but the number of people who actually put together these collections and make comparative grammars and language atlases – that's a dozen, two dozen. It's really not such a big community.

JMc: Did this community of language scholars work largely in isolation from other fields that were developing at the time, or are there interactions between linguistics and other sciences such as ethnography, psychology, history?

FS: Well, one of the greatest interactions that you haven't mentioned yet actually is with geography. One way of literally mapping the languages of the world is through language atlases, and the people who invent the language atlas are geographers. It's Adriano Balbi working in Paris who also makes an *Atlas ethnographique du globe*, which is actually an overview of the languages of the world, and it's Julius Klaproth, who is a self-taught Sinologist, who then turns to studying the languages of Asia and who also is a geographer, literally a map maker. In the Bibliothèque nationale in Paris there are hundreds of his map designs. For Julius Klaproth, there really is this strong intersection between linguistics and geography.

But ethnology is indeed the most direct sister of linguistics within this project of what I call the "mapping of the world", because language is one of the clearest denominators of ethnic boundaries on a non-political level. Everyone who studied languages in the nineteenth century was aware that the overlap was not complete, that you can also learn a language if you are not part of that people, but generally, a people and the language community are overlapping unities.

Of course, this notion of "people" was involved with all kinds of projections of their own, especially in German, *Volk*, but for the sake of making distinctions between different peoples, it makes sense. If your aim is to know what the main differences are between peoples in a particular region and how we should relate to them, then language really is the most common denominator. What you also see is that – and this of course is one of the dark heritages of the nineteenth-century colonial project – this classification is then reinforced or formulated in terms of physical anthropology, in terms of theories of race.

But one of the remarkable things here is that these scholars are aware that there are such things as miscegenation, both on a linguistic and on a racial level, and there also is actually far less consensus about racial classification than there is about linguistic classification. This is surprising, but people nowadays tend to talk about racial theory in the nineteenth century as if it is this one big dark thing, and it is pretty dark – I wouldn't want to deny that – but it's not one thing. There are something like half a dozen conflicting racial theories, and it is common knowledge that they are leaking on all sides. There are theories that simply divide people into different colours. Black, white, red, yellow, and maybe also brown. Or that divide them into different facial forms. Or that divide them by types of hair growth. That's actually the most comical one. It's Ernst Haeckel who comes up with it. He says that colour is an arbitrary standard because it changes depending on the climate. Physical proportions are a continuum. But the different hair types are discrete sets, so he divides people into those with sleek hair, and those with curly hair, and those with woolly hair.

JMc: And I believe that's the basis of Friedrich Müller's linguistic classification.

FS: Yes, so then you have these *wollhaarigen Sprachen*, a classification which really doesn't pass the giggle test.

JMc: I guess also that, by the end of the nineteenth century, scholars who were trying to come up with rigorous scientific definitions for racial theory found that it didn't stack up and eventually abandoned it.

FS: What you see indeed is that there is a growing awareness, at least within the scientific community, that these distinctions are somewhat arbitrary, but the practice still continues. Physical anthropology continues indeed until after World War II. What happens is that racial theory, because it is "natural science", has this sort of appeal as a more rigid quantitative approach. The practice continues even after Franz Boas starts not only noticing that the categories leak, but actively gathering lots of anthropometric data with the express aim of showing that anthropometry is not the right way to quantify people.

Another interesting example is Pater Wilhelm Schmidt, the man who basically represents Catholic ethnolinguistics, who writes an atlas of the world's languages, devises the classification of Australian Aboriginal languages that still more or less holds today, and reorganizes the collections of the Propaganda Fide into the Vatican Missionary-Ethnological Museum. Schmidt is firmly convinced you should look at culture, not race, but he says you should do that because ethnology is a separate scientific discipline. Meanwhile he also keeps treating racial theory as a fully bona fide scientific approach. So there is this oddly funny – well, it depends on your sense of humour – there is this very paradoxical outcome that he writes a tract *Rasse und Volk* in the 1920s, and then after the Nazis take over, he reformulates it into a longer tract: *Rasse und Volk. Ihre allgemeine Bedeutung, ihre Geltung im deutschen Raum* (Race and People: their General Meaning and their Significance in the German Area). In spite of its title, this book gets banned by the Nazis because what Schmidt says about the meaning of racial theories is that they are irrelevant for understanding what a people is and what a language is. Obviously, Pater Wilhelm Schmidt is not my hero – let's be clear about that – but he does represent a parting of the ways in this program.

JMc: Thanks very much, Floris, for talking to us about linguistic scholarship in the long nineteenth century.

FS: Thank you very much, James, for this service to the Republic of Letters.

Primary sources

Adelung, Johann Christoph & Johann Severin Vater. 1806–1817. *Mithridates, oder allgemeine Sprachenkunde.* Berlin: Vossische Buchhandlung.

Balbi, Adriano. 1826. *Atlas ethnographique du globe.* Paris.

Bleek, Wilhelm H. I. 1858–1859. Australia. In *The library of His Excellency Sir George Grey, K.C.B., philology.* London: Trübner & Co.

Boas, Franz. 1940. *Race, language, and culture.* New York: Macmillan.

Du Ponceau, Stephen Peter. 1838. *Mémoire sur le système grammatical des langues de quelques nations indiennes de l'Amerique du Nord.* Paris: Pihan de la Forest.

Grierson, George. 1903–1926. *The linguistic survey of India.* Calcutta: Govt. Printing House.

Haeckel, Ernst. 1868. *Natürliche Schöpfungsgeschichte: Gemeinverständliche wissenschaftliche Vorträge über die Entwickelungslehre im Allgemeinen und diejenige von Darwin, Goethe und Lamarck im Besonderen.* Berlin: Reimer.

Hervás y Panduro, Lorenzo. 1787a. *Saggio practicco delle lingue con prolegomeni e una raccolta di orazioni dominicali in più di trecento lingue e dialetti.* Cesena: Biasini.

Hervás y Panduro, Lorenzo. 1787b. *Vocabolario poliglotto, con prolegomeni sopra più de cl lingue.* Cesena: Biasini.

Humboldt, Wilhelm von. 1836. *Über die Verschiedenheit des menschlichen Sprachbaues: Über die Kawi-Sprache auf der Insel Java.* Alexander von Humboldt (ed.). Berlin: Dümmler.

Humboldt, Wilhelm von. 1988 [1836]. *On language. The diversity of human language structure and its influence on the mental development of mankind.* Trans. by Peter Heath. Cambridge: Cambridge University Press.

Klaproth, Julius. 1823. *Asia polyglotta.* Paris: Schubart.

Koelle, Sigismund. 1854. *Polyglotta africana.* London: Church Missionary House.

Lepsius, Karl Richard. 1854. *Das allgemeine linguistische Alphabet: Grundsätze der Übertragung fremder Schriftsysteme und bisher noch ungeschriebener Sprachen in europäische Buchstaben.* Berlin: Hertz.

Lepsius, Karl Richard. 1863. *Standard alphabet for reducing unwritten languages and foreign graphic systems to a uniform orthography in European letters.* London: Williams & Norgate.

Marsden, William. 1782. Remarks on the Sumatran languages. In a letter to Sir Joseph Banks, Bart. President of the Royal Society. *Archaeologia* VI. 154–158.

Marsden, William. 1827. *Bibliotheca marsdeniana philologica et orientalis: A catalogue of books and manuscripts, collected with a view to the general comparison of languages, and to the study of oriental literature.* London: Cox.

Müller, Friedrich. 1876. *Grundriß der Sprachwissenschaft.* Vol. 4. Vienna: Hölder.

Raffles, Thomas Stamford. 1830 [1817]. *The history of Java.* London: Murray.

Schlegel, Friedrich. 1808. *Ueber die Sprache und Weisheit der Indier.* Heidelberg: Mohr und Zimmer.

Schlegel, Friedrich. 1900 [1808]. On the Indian language, literature and philosophy. In E. J. Millington (ed.), *The æsthetic and miscellaneous works of Friedrich von Schlegel*, 425–536. London: George Bell.

Schmidt, Wilhelm. 1919. *Die Gliederung der australischen Sprachen.* Vienna: Mechitaristen-Verlag.

Schmidt, Wilhelm. 1926. *Die Sprachfamilien und Sprachenkreise der Erde.* Heidelberg: Winter.

Schmidt, Wilhelm. 1927. *Rasse und Volk. Eine Untersuchung zur Bestimmung ihrer Grenzen und zur Erfassung ihrer Beziehungen.* München: Kösel und Pustet.

Secondary sources

Alter, Stephen. 1999. *Darwinism and the linguistic image: Language, race, and natural theology in the nineteenth century.* Baltimore: Johns Hopkins.

Daston, Lorraine & Catherine Park. 2006. Introduction: The age of the new. In Lorraine Daston & Catherine Park (eds.), *The Cambridge history of science.* Cambridge: Cambridge University Press.

Majeed, Javed. 2018. *Colonialism and knowledge in Grierson's Linguistic Survey of India.* London: Routledge.

Marchand, Suzanne. 2003. Priests among the Pygmies: Wilhelm Schmidt and the counter-reformation in Austrian ethnology. In H. G. Penny & M. Bunzl (eds.), *Worldly provincialism: German anthropology in the age of empire*, 283–316. Ann Arbor: University of Michigan Press.

McNeely, Ian. 2020. The last project of the Republic of Letters: Wilhelm von Humboldt's global linguistics. *Journal of Modern History* 92. 241–273.

Messling, Markus. 2016. *Gebeugter Geist – Rassismus und Erkenntnis in der modernen europäischen Philologie.* Göttingen: Wallstein.

Shapin, Steven. 1996. *The Scientific Revolution*. Chicago: University of Chicago Press.

Solleveld, Floris. 2016. How to make a revolution. Revolutionary rhetoric in the humanities around 1800. *History of Humanities* 1(2). 277–301.

Solleveld, Floris. 2019. Language, people, and maps: the ethnolinguistics of George Grierson and Franz Boas [review essay]. *History of Humanities* 4(2). 461–471.

Solleveld, Floris. 2020a. Afterlives of the Republic of Letters. Learned journals and scholarly community in the early 19th century. *Erudition and the Republic of Letters* 5(1). 82–116.

Solleveld, Floris. 2020b. Expanding the comparative view: Humboldt's Über die Kawi-Sprache and its language materials. *Historiographia Linguistica* 47(1). 52–82.

Solleveld, Floris. 2020c. Klaproth, Balbi, and the Language Atlas. In Emilie Aussant & Jean-Michel Fortis (eds.), *History of linguistics 2017: Selected papers from the 14th International Conference on the History of the Language Sciences (ICHoLS XIV)*, 81–99. Amsterdam: John Benjamins.

Solleveld, Floris. 2020d. Language gathering and philological expertise: Sigismund Koelle, Wilhelm Bleek, and the languages of africa". In Jacques François (ed.), *Les linguistes allemands du XIXème siècle et leurs interlocuteurs étrangers*, 169–200. Paris: Éditions de la Société de Linguistique de Paris.

Solleveld, Floris. 2020e. Lepsius as a linguist: Fieldwork, philology, phonetics, and the "Hamitic hypothesis". *Language and History* 63(3). 193–213.

Chapter 4

Ferdinand de Saussure

John E. Joseph[a] & James McElvenny[b]
[a]University of Edinburgh [b]University of Siegen

JMc: In this interview, we're joined by John Joseph, Professor of Applied Linguistics at the University of Edinburgh. He'll be talking to us about the great Genevan linguist Ferdinand de Saussure. John is the author of many works relevant to our topic today, the most significant of which would have to be his 2012 biography of Saussure, published with Oxford University Press.

So, John, please tell us about Saussure. Saussure is perhaps best known for his *Course in general linguistics*, which is widely considered a foundational text of linguistic structuralism. What's your view on this matter? Would you say that Saussure's *Course* was a truly groundbreaking work that single-handedly brought structuralism into being?

JEJ: For my part, James, I'm still struggling to understand what "structuralism" meant and means. The linguists who called their approach structural weren't all doing the same thing; they agreed on some principles and vigorously disputed others. One thing they shared was an impulse to analyse and write about languages in a way that was modern – modernist even – and in the *Course in general linguistics* they found a model for doing that. Nothing about language and intelligence, or language and the national soul, or culture, and an out-and-out rejection of any connection of language with race. No deep philosophical ruminations. Some later structuralists would make links with philosophy, and vice versa. But for linguists, whatever philosophical implications may have been latent in the *Course* could be left aside, and they could focus on its very sleek, minimalist model of a system of linguistic signs, each made up of a value – a

John E. Joseph & James McElvenny. 2022. Ferdinand de Saussure. In James McElvenny (ed.), *Interviews in the history of linguistics: Volume I*, 41–49. Berlin: Language Science Press. DOI: 10.5281/zenodo.7096294 value that was purely its difference from the other elements in the system. That's modernist, and especially in the wake of World War I, when there was a desire to move forward in a new scientific direction, it had great appeal.

JMc: What influence did Saussure's *Course* have on linguistic scholarship of the time? So the Prague School certainly appealed to Saussure quite often, but did they really follow him? And what about their contemporaries in the English-speaking world, such as Leonard Bloomfield and Edward Sapir in the US or even John Rupert Firth in England?

JEJ: I'll start with the Prague School, and Roman Jakobson, who introduced the term structuralism as a literary and linguistic method or approach. No one did more to disseminate Saussure's *Course* and proclaim its fundamental importance than Jakobson did – and there was hardly any position taken by Saussure that Jakobson didn't contest, or even reject out of hand. That includes the fundamental precept that linguistic signs are purely differential. Saussurean phonology is what's nowadays called a "substance-free" phonology, where it's all about patterns in the mind, and the sounds don't matter. Jakobson and his collaborator Nikolai Trubetzkoy said no, some sounds in a language are very distinctive to the ear, whilst others are harder to distinguish, and those maximally distinctive sounds are in various respects more fundamental.

Jakobson wrote an article called "Why 'mama' and 'papa'?", why across the world's languages is it disproportionately the case that /m/ and /p/ or /b/, and the vowel /a/, figure in the words by which children call the two most important people in their lives? The answer lies for Jakobson in the maximal distinctiveness of these sounds to the ear, making them the easiest and first sounds for children to master, to produce systematically. A sound such as /θ/ is hard to distinguish from /s/ or /f/ or /tʰ/, and it's no coincidence that /θ/ is relatively rare amongst the world's languages, is learned late by children and is unstable over time. The number which follows two is *three* for me, but *tree* in many Irish dialects, and *free* in a growing number of English dialects. Saussurean phonology can't account for this; all it can say is that /θ/ is a phoneme by virtue of its difference from /s/, /f/ and /t/ – degrees of difference don't enter into the equation. So here Jakobson directly contradicts Saussure on a fundamental matter – yet Jakobson was always the first to say that only because of Saussure's *Course* was he able to make this step at all.

Prague wasn't the only place where structural linguistics was moving forward in the 1920s and '30s. Louis Hjelmslev had left Copenhagen to study with Saussure's former pupil Antoine Meillet in Paris, and Hjelmslev's 1928 book *Principes de grammaire générale* is deeply Saussurean in orientation. So is the first volume of his next book, *La catégorie des cas* from 1935 – but by the second volume, two years later, he's come into the orbit of Jakobson, and from then on the Copenhagen School's relationship to Saussure is comparable to Jakobson's own, where Saussure is revered as the founding figure who has made it possible for them to move beyond what he himself taught. In Paris, too, Émile Benveniste's efforts at the end of the 1960s to extend linguistics beyond the semiotic are characterized as simultaneously surpassing and accomplishing Saussure's project.

With Sapir and Bloomfield, Saussure's *Course* figures in their writings starting already in the 1920s. Frustrated at criticism of his book *Language* for not citing Saussure more, Bloomfield wrote to one of his students that Saussure's influence is on every page. Sapir, as an anthropologist, had been well prepared for Saussurean linguistics through his work with Franz Boas, whose 1911 *Handbook of American Indian languages* shares the modernist spirit of Saussure's *Course*. On the other hand, Sapir wanted to extend his linguistic enquiry into the psychological dimension, whereas Saussure resolutely left psychology to the psychologists. Not that he dismissed it, by any means; but he'd been brought up with constant admonitions to choose a particular discipline and not stray beyond it. Saussure's expertise was as a "grammarian", as he usually called himself; any view he might venture on the psychology of language would be nothing more than opinion, not expertise, and could only damage his scholarly reputation.

Finally, you asked about J. R. Firth. My emeritus colleague Ron Asher, Firth's student, tells me that he can't recall a single lecture by Firth in which Saussure wasn't discussed. In 1950 Firth wrote that all linguists were now defined as Saussureans, anti-Saussureans, post-Saussureans, or non-Saussureans. Firth himself somehow managed to be all four. The *system* – that was the crucial thing Firth took from Saussure, but Saussure, in his modernist impulse, had pared the system down to something oversimplified. Firth set out to rectify this, with systems within systems, tiered systems: and a concern with including linguistic *meaning* within the system, not just in the sense of the "signified", that part of the linguistic sign which is conceptual but internal to the language. Meaning *beyond* language – what connects language to the people who speak it, them to one another and to the world they inhabit. Again, what Saussure cut off as lying beyond what he as a grammarian was qualified to talk about. It was the business of philosophers, psychologists and other specialists. For Firth, as for Ogden and Richards in their book *The meaning of meaning*, that would always be Saussure's great limitation.

JMc: What then are the innovative features of Saussure's *Course* and why do you think it has been elevated to this status akin to that of holy scripture?

JEJ: "Holy scripture" is an exaggeration, to put it mildly! Much of the innova-
tion lies, as I've said, in what it doesn't talk about, or pushes out of the centre and
into the hinterland of the later chapters. At the centre it puts the linguistic sign,
and that's always been received as the most innovative aspect. Saussure defines
a language as a system of linguistic signs – not sounds, or words, or sentences,
not as something that, because it's always evolving, has no stable existence that
would allow it to be the subject of scientific enquiry in terms of what it is and
how it works at a given time.

None of these issues is ignored – rather, they're laid out as alternative ways of
analysing a language. And crucially, Saussure points out that the way you study
it actually determines what the nature is of the thing you're studying. He said:
"the point of view determines the object". You can study the system, *la langue*,
the socially shared language, or you can study utterances and texts, *la parole*, the
speech of an individual. Both are valid, and each is necessary for an understanding of the other. You can study them across time, diachronically, or at a moment
in time, synchronically.

Other linguists hadn't been mapping out the field of study in this widescreen
way, with all these options. They proclaimed *the* way – and so entrenched was
this mindset that the *Course* was widely read as if it too fit that pattern. As if
Saussure was saying that linguistics had to be about *langue*, not *parole*, had to be
synchronic, not diachronic. That he denied any link between linguistic signifieds
and things in the world, referents in Frege's terms – when he simply left that to
philosophers and psychologists to deal with as their specialized domain.

In terms of style, too, the *Course* is innovative in deriving from lectures, and
only in part from the author's own lecture notes. As is well known, students'
notes from the three academic years over which he gave the lectures were collated, and a plan was made based mainly on how things were arranged in the last
version of the course. Saussure had been trying and failing to write books about
big methodological questions in the study of languages since his early 20s. The
problem was that he was a perfectionist, determined that every word from his
pen had to be precisely the right word – hence the thousands of draft manuscript
pages in his archives that lay unpublished until recent years, in which the same
thought is often recomposed ten, twenty times, then scratched through and abandoned.

If he had written the *Course in general linguistics* – if he could have written it
– it might have been as turgid a book as the one on the primitive Indo-European
vowel system which made his reputation at the age of 21, but which only a relatively small number of specialists have ever managed to work their way through.
The posthumous *Course* is quite the opposite – not the easiest book to read, but

neither is every claim nailed down with a fixity that would protect it from any quibble. It's a very open text – it invites readers into a world of ideas and questions in which they can make their own interpretations and give their own answers. Hence its eventual popularity, though that didn't come until 50 years after it was published. The price of its textual openness and popularity is of course that it gets read very differently by different people, hence the large amount of scholarly work aimed at trying to understand what Saussure actually thought, which in many cases remains a mystery.

JMc: Do you think it would be fair to say that Saussure was simply perpetuating – and perhaps refining, but essentially perpetuating – ideas and methods that were already current among the generation of his teachers, the Neogrammarians?

JEJ: No, it would unsustainable to assert that Saussure was just teaching what everyone else was saying at the time. The academic economy demands continuity; anyone who tries to teach or write something without starting from the status quo of academic authority wouldn't be hailed as a revolutionary, but banished as a crackpot. It's a common enough game to point to the continuities and say, look, Freud said nothing that Charcot wasn't already teaching, just sexed-up. So you get Eugenio Coseriu, for instance, claiming in 1967 that all of Saussure is already there in Georg von der Gabelentz – nothing against Gabelentz, a great linguist, but it's as easy to build a case based just on the continuities as it is a counter-case based on the differences.

   If we want to make a realistic historical assessment of how Saussure's linguistics relates to the ideas and models of the Neogrammarians, we should look first at how Saussure's *Course* was received by the linguists of the time, who after all were mostly practising the methods laid down by the Neogrammarians. In their eyes, what Saussure taught embodied a sea change from accepted ideas. That starts with his two colleagues who edited the *Course*, Albert Sechehaye and Charles Bally – in fact, it started before them, with the students whom Saussure taught in his first job, in Paris from 1881 to 1891. They included Antoine Meillet, who always credited Saussure as creator of the radically new linguistic analysis which, led in Paris by Meillet, would develop into structuralism.

   Book reviewers of the *Course* hailed its novelty, whilst also seizing upon links to their own ideas when they could be used to strengthen their position – thus you see Leonard Bloomfield in 1924 claiming that Saussure's signifier and signified are in effect the stimulus and response of the behaviourism that Bloomfield himself had begun to follow. Again, I've stressed how the modernism of the

Course contributed to it sweeping away existing doctrines, including those of the Neogrammarians, which had acquired that musty smell that forty-year-old ideas get. But it wasn't the case that Saussure had recycled them in a new rhetorical dress and with some refinements. Just look at the core Saussurean concept of the language system as a system of values as pure difference, divorced from their phonetic realization – when phonetic physicality is at the heart of Neogrammarian "sound laws", with the psychological phenomenon of analogy admitted as a necessary explanatory escape hatch. For Saussure, the reverse: analogy, as mental processing, is placed at the centre, and phonetics becomes an adjunct to linguistics. So no wonder the *Course* had the impact it did.

JMc: So in these cases where Saussure broke with his contemporaries and immediate predecessors, would you say that the alternative ideas he put forward were novel or that he was just drawing on even older ideas that had been forgotten or were considered superseded in the academic linguistics of the late nineteenth century?

JEJ: Again, we mustn't forget the forces of academic economy, which demand that novel ideas be grounded in established authority: the classic example is Noam Chomsky's *Cartesian linguistics*, in which he claims that his transformational-generative linguistics is restoring the great seventeenth-century tradition of understanding language and mind, after its illegitimate usurpation by linguists after Wilhelm von Humboldt. The *Course in general linguistics* accomplished something similar, though without any overt claim to be doing so. Chomsky's "Cartesians" weren't really connected to Descartes, but never mind – his principal heroes were Lancelot and Arnauld, authors of the Port-Royal Grammar and Logic, which laid out the idea of a *grammaire générale*, a universal grammar. This became established in French education, and over the course of the eighteenth century it came to include as one of its key components the idea of the linguistic sign, the conjunction of a signifying sound or set of sounds, and a signified concept, joined arbitrarily, which is to say with no necessary "natural" link of sound to concept.

In France, the *grammaire générale* tradition in education, by which I mean secondary education, didn't survive the Napoleonic period, when virtually everything was reformed. However, Geneva, whilst French-speaking, isn't France, and the *grammaire générale* tradition didn't get reformed out of education in Geneva until much later. The young Saussure was in the last cohort of students taught by venerable men in their 70s who had been trained in *grammaire générale* in the first third of the century, and included the theory of linguistic signs in their courses. It was something he and his age-mates had all been taught, and perhaps took to be common sense. In any case, he certainly didn't imagine that when he included it in his courses in general linguistics almost forty years later that anyone would think it was his original idea. If so he would have pointed out its historical legacy, going back to antiquity. As fate would have it, that legacy was sufficiently forgotten that all but a few readers of the *Course* experienced its theory of the linguistic sign as something radically new and modern.

This part of the *Course* is one that had a very strong impact, perhaps the strongest, across a vast range of fields. But the theory of signs in the *Course* becomes radically different from any that went before when he adds in the dimension that signifiers aren't sounds, and signifieds aren't things; he formulates them as mental patterns, sound patterns and concepts; but even this isn't the definitive formulation, just something his students can get their head around more easily than they could with what is his ultimate view – namely, that each signifier is a value generated by difference from every other signifier within the same system, just as each signified is a value generated by difference from every other signified. That's a core example of what makes the *Course in general linguistics* unique. To every question you ask me about whether it draws on earlier ideas or is novel, the answer is: 100% both, somehow. Which is impossible. And OK, perhaps that's what makes your sacred scripture analogy tempting: this book defies explanation. Its own author couldn't write it. It was assembled from notes from three courses over which ideas were evolving and shifting, and were jotted down by various students in often incompatible ways. The editors did their best, but got some important things wrong, and the book isn't devoid of internal contradictions. Yet somehow the result was extraordinary. You might even say miraculous.

JMc: Ah. Well, thanks very much for talking to us about Saussure. I'm sure you've inspired many of our listeners to go out there and read more about him.

JEJ: Thanks very much, James.

Primary sources

Arnauld, Antoine & Claude Lancelot. 1660. *Grammaire générale et raisonnée*. Paris: Pierre le Petit.

Arnauld, Antoine & Claude Lancelot. 1975 [1660]. *General and rational grammar: The Port-Royal Grammar.* Trans. by Jacques Rieux & Bernard E. Rollin. The Hague: Mouton.

Benveniste, Émile. 2012. *Dernières leçons: Collège de France, 1968 et 1969.* Jean-Claude Coquet & Irène Fenoglio (eds.). Paris: École des Hautes Études en Sciences Sociales, Gallimard, Seuil.

Benveniste, Émile. 2019. *Last lectures: Collège de France, 1968 and 1969.* Jean-Claude Coquet & Irène Fenoglio (eds.). Trans. by John E. Joseph. Edinburgh: Edinburgh University Press.

Bloomfield, Leonard. 1924. Review of Saussure (1922). *Modern Language Journal* 8. 317–319. DOI: 10.2307/313991.

Bloomfield, Leonard. 1933. *Language.* New York: Henry Holt.

Boas, Franz. 1911. *Handbook of American Indian languages.* Vol. 1. Washington, D.C.: Government Printing Office.

Firth, John Rupert. 1950. Personality and language in society. *Sociological Review* 42. 37–52.

Hjelmslev, Louis. 1928. *Principes de grammaire générale.* Copenhagen: Munksgaard.

Hjelmslev, Louis. 1935–1937. *La catégorie des cas. Étude de grammaire générale.* Aarhus: Universitetsforlaget.

Jakobson, Roman. 1962 [1959]. Why "mama" and "papa"? In *Selected writings, vol. I: Phonological studies*, 538–545. The Hague: Mouton de Gruyter.

Jakobson, Roman. 1971 [1929]. Retrospect. In *Selected writings, vol. II: Word and language*, 711–722. The Hague: Mouton de Gruyter.

Meillet, Antoine. 1921–1936. *Linguistique historique et linguistique générale.* Paris: Champion.

Ogden, Charles K. & Ivor A. Richards. 1949 [1923]. *The meaning of meaning: A study of the influence of language upon thought and the science of symbolism.* London: Routledge.

Saussure, Ferdinand de. 1879. *Mémoire sur le système primitif des voyelles dans les langues indo-européennes.* Leipzig: B. G. Teubner.

Saussure, Ferdinand de. 1922 [1916]. *Cours de linguistique générale.* Charles Bally & Albert Sechehaye (eds.). 2nd ed. Paris: Payot.

Saussure, Ferdinand de. 1959 [1916]. *Course in general linguistics.* Trans. by Wade Baskin. New York: Philosophical Library.

Secondary sources

Chomsky, Noam. 2009 [1966]. *Cartesian linguistics: A chapter in the history of rationalist thought.* James McGilvray (ed.). Cambridge: Cambridge University Press.

Coseriu, Eugenio. 1967. Georg von der Gabelentz et la linguistique synchronique. *Word* 23. 74–110.

Joseph, John E. 2012. *Saussure.* Oxford: Oxford University Press.

Joseph, John E. 2017. Ferdinand de Saussure. *Oxford Research Encyclopedia of Linguistics.* DOI: 10.1093/acrefore/9780199384655.013.385.

Joseph, John E. 2020. Structure, mentalité, société, civilisation : les quatre linguistiques d'antoine meillet. In *Shs web of conferences 78.* https://www.shs-conferences.org/articles/shsconf/abs/2020/06/shsconf_cmlf2020_15002/shsconf_cmlf2020_15002.html.

McElvenny, James. 2017. Georg von der Gabelentz. *Oxford Research Encyclopedia of Linguistics.* DOI: 10.1093/acrefore/9780199384655.013.379.

McElvenny, James. 2018. *Language and meaning in the age of modernism: C. K. Ogden and his contemporaries.* Edinburgh: Edinburgh University Press.

Chapter 5

The emergence of phonetics as a field

Michael Ashby[a] & James McElvenny[b]

[a]University College London [b]University of Siegen

JMc: In this interview, we're joined by phonetician and historian of linguistics Michael Ashby. Michael is a former Senior Lecturer in Phonetics at University College London, the current President of the International Phonetic Association, and the Treasurer of the Henry Sweet Society for the History of Linguistic Ideas. He's going to talk to us about the history of phonetics from the nineteenth century to the early twentieth century.

So, Michael, can you tell us about the beginnings of modern phonetic scholarship? When did the modern field of phonetics begin to emerge, and how did it fit in with the intellectual and academic landscape of the time? Was it primarily a pure field interested in the accumulation of knowledge for its own sake, or was it more applied, connected to language teaching, orthography reform and so on?

MA: The nineteenth century was when phonetics became clearly defined and got a name. It grew up at the intersection of linguistic science with two other fields. One of them is mathematics and physical science, chiefly acoustics, and the other, medical science, especially physiology. If we start with physiology, there had been over centuries an accumulating body of knowledge about the articulation of speech, but there were also many bizarre misconceptions. The nineteenth century was when scientific medicine really got going, and it was only to be expected that physiologists would turn their attention to the speech organs, especially the larynx, and there were big steps in the early nineteenth century.

Michael Ashby & James McElvenny. 2022. The emergence of phonetics as a field. In James McElvenny (ed.), *Interviews in the history of linguistics: Volume I*, 51–60. Berlin: Language Science Press. DOI: 10.5281/zenodo.7096296

A very significant event for linguists was the publication of von Brücke's *Grundzüge der Physiologie* in 1856, because von Brücke is the person who gets articulatory phonetics more or less right for the first time. For instance, he drew separate vocal tract diagrams illustrating the production of various sounds, just like those in a modern phonetics text. You could use them today. Well, his book was soon joined by others, and von Brücke himself went to a second edition later in the century. So long story cut short, but that's the physiological background.

Turning to mathematics and acoustics, it's a parallel story, really. Again, ancient antecedents, but rapid ground-breaking advances in the early nineteenth century, new light thrown on vowel production, the nature of resonance, and in 1863, Hermann Helmholtz published his great work *Die Lehre von den Tonempfindungen*. That's to say, the science of sensations of tone. It's a comprehensive work on sound, covering analysis, synthesis, hearing, and taking into account the sounds of speech.

Helmholtz was translated into English by Alexander Ellis, a pioneer phonetician who in his day was President of the Philological Society. So he brings us to the third component: linguistic science itself. It was linguists, really, who defined the scope of the subject and gave it a name. The noun "phonetics" as the name for a field of study started to be used in the 1840s, and in the 1870s, two particularly significant and closely contemporary linguistic phoneticians came to the fore: in Germany, Eduard Sievers, and in Britain, Henry Sweet, and their major phonetics handbooks appeared in successive years: 1876, 1877.

You ask about pure or applied research. Well, as often I think it was both. Certainly, practical applications were never far away. The teaching of the deaf had been a goal for centuries. Von Brücke's *Physiologie* explicitly says in the title that it's for linguists and teachers of the deaf. As for orthography reform, yes, many phoneticians were also advocates of spelling reform. Sweet's 1877 *Handbook of Phonetics* has a sizeable appendix devoted to the topic, and some phoneticians kept up this interest well into the twentieth century. As for the connection of phonetics with language teaching, that became particularly important in the last quarter of the nineteenth century because of the Reform Movement.

An excellent contemporary view of the development of phonetics and its place in the intellectual and scientific climate of the time can be got from one of Max Müller's *Lectures on the Science of Language* delivered in 1863. It's called 'The Physiological Alphabet'. Müller identifies the same three contributing fields exactly as I did just now, so he's read von Brücke and Helmholtz, and he knows the writings of Ellis, but it's all new and exciting and unfolding around him at the point when he's writing, and he's interpreting it for the Royal Institution audience. It's a brilliant piece and must have done a great deal to popularize the idea of phonetics in the mid-nineteenth century.

JMc: So what role do you think advances in recording and other sound technology played in the development of phonetics as a science in the nineteenth century?

MA: Developments in technology did play a very significant role, though maybe not in the way your question might suggest, at least not at first, because the actual accumulation of archives of recorded language samples on any scale doesn't begin until the early twentieth century.

The earliest device which picked up sound and did something with it was the phonautograph. It draws waveforms. It's a primitive oscillograph. It was announced in 1859, and it was almost immediately put to use in speech research. People had wondered whether vowels were characterized by what we now call formants – that is, resonances determined by the vocal tract position – or by specific harmonics – that is, fixed characteristics of the voice at a given pitch. The Dutch physiologist Donders analysed some vowel waveforms and reached the correct conclusion that the quality of vowels is determined by what he called overtones with a characteristic frequency, and that's what we'd now call formants.

The phonautograph draws pictures, but it can't play the sounds back; that came in 1877, when Edison announced the phonograph. Now people were quick to see that if the microscopic phonograph groove could somehow be enlarged for examination, a great deal could be learnt about the speech signal. By July of the following year, two British engineers, Jenkin and Ewing, published a substantial report in which they described their method of enlarging the groove 400 times, and they subject the resulting waveforms to quantitative harmonic analysis. What they're describing in 1878 just a few months after the invention of the phonograph is now the very basis of all work in acoustic analysis of speech, though now, of course, a computer performs all the calculations they had to do laboriously by hand.

It's not only sound recording devices, but other instruments and techniques began to be applied to speech. In 1872, a London dentist, James Oakley Coles, described the technique we now call palatography. He painted the upper surface of the mouth with a mixture of flour and gum, made a single articulation, and then used a mirror to look at the wipe-off pattern showing tongue contact. Others refined the technique; later it became more usual to use an artificial palate which could be removed for easier examination. Around the same time, 1876, the kymograph, which was a physiological recording device, was first applied to the study of dynamic speech movements.

Instruments became altogether more numerous, and in 1891, Rousselot submitted a ground-breaking dissertation using a whole battery of instruments together to investigate his own variety of French. It was widely regarded as epoch-making, and those who enthusiastically followed his lead explicitly say that they were participating in a paradigm shift.

From the 1890s onwards, therefore, there has been something of a division – Sweet's word was "antagonism" – between traditional linguistic ear phonetics on one side and laboratory-based experimental phonetics on the other. In my view, it is to a large degree a manufactured division, a manufactured antagonism, but that's another story.

JMc: What connections were there in the nineteenth century and the early twentieth century between phonetic scholarship and linguistic theory in such areas as historical-comparative linguistics, the documentation of non-European languages, and general linguistics? Did phoneticians pay attention to work in these areas, and did linguists take note of advances in phonetic science in formulating their theories?

MA: Just how and why phonetics matters is set out brilliantly in the first few lines of Sweet's *Handbook* of 1877. That's where he famously describes phonetics, and this is a quote, as "the indispensable foundation of all study of language, whether theoretical or practical." The fact is that phonetics was absolutely central to the comparative-historical enterprise, which is after all founded on regular sound correspondences. As Sweet says, "Without phonetics," and this is another quote from him, "philology, whether comparative or historical, is mere mechanical enumeration of letter changes."

As the century went on, I think the importance of phonetics as the explanatory basis of language variation and change just grew and grew. If we go back to von Brücke's *Grundzüge der Physiologie*, yes, he was a physiologist, but it wasn't that he wrote a physiology text which then just turned out to be useful to linguists. He knew several languages himself, he had an interest in linguistic theory, he had friends who were active in Indo-European linguistics. He deliberately set out to produce a physiology text to provide the basis for linguistic science.

Similarly with Sievers later in the century. Sievers himself was a Neogrammarian. He even has an Indo-European sound law named after him, Sievers' Law, and his phonetics manual is number one in a series devoted to Indo-European grammars. It was planned as the foundation of the whole thing. I think at the end of the century, the Neogrammarians' phonetics reading list is just those two, von Brücke and Sievers.

Now, the role of phonetics in documenting unwritten languages is, again, something stressed in the opening lines of Sweet's 1877 *Handbook*. There were two interesting major efforts in the nineteenth century in the direction of producing a universal notation system that would be suitable for dealing with unwritten languages. One is the Prix Volney, a prize essay series given in accordance with the terms of a bequest, where – to begin with, at least – the question posed by the committee of judges was precisely that of creating a universal alphabet. This produced a series of analyses and proposals from 1822 onwards. Now, the motivation for the Prix Volney is general linguistic inquiry into whether such an alphabet was feasible, and many of the answers are rather philosophical in character.

Another important impetus came from the Protestant missionary effort. Here, the focus is not on language documentation as an end in itself, but as a means to the spreading of Christianity and translation of the Gospel. In 1854, the so-called 'Alphabetical Conferences' were held in London. Actually, in modern terms, it was one conference. What was plural was sessions on three days within a week. They were organised by Christian Karl Bunsen, who was a Prussian diplomat and scholar living in London, and he invited a galaxy of leading scientists, scholars, and churchmen to a high-powered brainstorming session, really, on the question of developing the universal alphabet for missionary use.

Max Müller was one of those attending, and he presented his own candidate missionary alphabet, although it wasn't adopted. Another participant was the Prussian linguist and Egyptologist Karl Richard Lepsius, who presented the first form of his Standard Alphabet. Eventually, a revised version of that alphabet was published in English with funding from the Church Missionary Society and did see fairly widespread use, especially in Africa, and it was adopted indeed by some general linguists – Whitney, for example.

The truth is, though, that a great deal of language documentation throughout the nineteenth century and into the twentieth was done without a good phonetic foundation. It's not so much the lack of a uniform notation that matters. It's lack of practical phonetic training and awareness, so that observers just fail to notice important features of the languages they're dealing with.

That's coupled with prejudice, too, about what could and could not be likely features of languages. The most graphic example of that I can give you is Max Müller on clicks at the Alphabetical Conferences. Clicks are a problem if you're making an alphabet. You don't have enough letters left over to deal with them.

What shall you do? Well, Müller's solution was not to symbolize them, but to abolish them. After all, there are African languages nearby that haven't got them, so they can't be necessary. And they are barbarous noises. "Barbarous" is the word he uses. So he seriously suggests that under the civilizing influence of the missionaries, speakers of the languages in question may be induced to give up the clicks.

JMc: Can you tell us about the founding of the International Phonetic Association? What was the impetus behind it, and what was the mission of the Association in its early years? How has this changed up to the present? I guess one of the most surprising things about the society is the nature of its journal. Since 1970, it's had the very academic and matter-of-fact title *Journal of the International Phonetic Association*, but prior to that it was called *The Phonetic Teacher* and then *Le Maître Phonétique*. Perhaps even more remarkable is the fact that up until 1970, everything in the journal was printed in the International Phonetic Alphabet. What happened in 1970, and what do these changes say about the evolving character of phonetics as a field?

MA: Yes, well, while the question of a universal alphabet remained unresolved, there were by the 1870s very viable phonetic notations – at least for English and other major European languages – using Latin letters and in many ways very similar to the phonetic alphabet we use today. The IPA came into existence not from the desire to create a new notation so much, but from a movement to use this already existing type of phonetic notation in the teaching of modern languages.

IPA means two things: the International Phonetic Alphabet, yes, but also the International Phonetic Association. It was an association that came first in 1886, but it wasn't actually called the International Phonetic Association until 1897. Before that, it was the Phonetic Teachers' Association, and the original membership was just a handful of teachers of English in Paris. The driving force behind this group was a young teacher called Paul Passy.

They'd all been inspired by a new trend in language teaching, the one we call the Reform Movement, and that had been launched on its way in 1882, just previously, with a rousing manifesto by Wilhelm Viëtor. He called for a complete change of direction in language teaching, and he was quickly supported by leading figures such as Henry Sweet who had himself not long previously called for reform of what he termed the "wretched" system of studying modern languages then in wide use.

Now, the use of phonetic transcription in teaching was an important plank of this new approach. The membership of the group snowballed, and members joined from around the world, most of them being schoolteachers. At the same time, leading linguists were members. Jespersen and Sweet had been members right from the beginning, and others joined. Interestingly, de Saussure joined in 1891, and he remained a member until his death. Now, while they were certainly interested in language teaching, figures like Sweet and Jespersen also had bigger concerns.

Right from the start, Jespersen tried to steer the Association in the direction of an international phonetic association, and he had Sweet's support, but it took more than 10 years before the ordinary membership agreed to the change. The Association's journal, *Le Maître Phonétique*, which had begun as a sort of homely newsletter, started to include articles and reviews that were more theoretical and unlikely to be of any direct use to a language teacher in a school.

Over time, the Association's aims and practices have evolved, and the constituency from which the membership is drawn has changed correspondingly. The teaching of modern languages went on being identified as one of the Association's leading priorities well into the twentieth century, but it began to fade as the century went on, and if you look through today's membership, you probably wouldn't find any modern language schoolteachers at all.

And yes, as you say, from the beginning right up until 1970, everything in the journal was printed in phonetic script – not just the language samples meant for reading practice, but the editorial matter, book reviews, obituaries, even the Association's financial reports. This is partly because many of the early supporters were also advocates of spelling reform, though the Association never did throw its weight behind any specific proposals for spelling reform in the way that it did ultimately formulate and promote its own phonetic alphabet.

By the mid-twentieth century, the use of phonetic script in the journal had become as much a habit as anything else. It was an eccentricity in some people's minds, and spelling reform, by this stage, I think, was a lost cause. My own view would be that it was a lost cause all along, but mid-twentieth century, it was an eccentric affection to use phonetic script for everything, and in the late 1960s, the IPA's governing council voted to drop the use of phonetic script in the journal and at the same time to change the title of the journal to *Journal of the International Phonetic Association*. Those changes came into force in 1971, and that's where we are today.

JMc: With the use of phonetic script for writing articles in the journal, was it a phonemic transcription of the language that the article was written in, or was it a much narrower phonetic transcription representing the accent of the author of the article?

MA: Well, I recommend you to have a look. It's all kinds of things and many different languages. The most extraordinary thing ever published, I think, is an article reviewing a book on Spanish, but the article is written in Welsh, transcribed Welsh – and if you think you know French or German, reading it in an experimental transcription from the late nineteenth century is great fun. So trying to make out what Viëtor is saying in transcription is a real test.

It's not quite true to say that it's in transcription. I used the word "phonetic script". I'm following what Mike MacMahon did. Most people who contributed were using phonetics as a kind of writing system. It's not that they're transcribing speech. They're doing written language, but they're using phonetic symbols rather than conventional orthography, so it's mixed in with ordinary punctuation. Numbers are written just with numbers. If a student were to put the date as "2021" in a transcription, it would be a mistake today, but they wrote numbers just using Arabic numerals. And they used quotes and italics and all kinds of devices of written language. They just didn't use ordinary spelling. But different people tried out different transcriptions, and indeed some transcription systems were first trialled in the journal. People tried them out to see how they worked, see what kind of a reaction they got.

JMc: So were the authors given free rein?

MA: I think so, yes.

JMc: So the editors of the journal didn't try to standardize the use of the phonetic alphabet.

MA: They did not try to standardize. I've looked for evidence of that. Rousselot, you know, who I've mentioned as the originator of the idea of a phonetics laboratory, was allowed by Passy, who was the editor of the journal, to print an article in the journal that was not in phonetic script. Rousselot thought the IPA was wrong in this, and Passy allowed him this rare privilege of writing in ordinary orthography. There's a bit by Scripture, who was an American, and yet the transcription looks suspiciously British, so there's a case where I think maybe a British phonetician at UCL had possibly transcribed a bit of ordinary text that Scripture had submitted, but apart from that, no, people were given free rein.

And sometimes it's Italian. Sometimes it's Spanish. Sometimes it's German. French was the official language of the Association until 1970 again. There were a few articles in French published even after that date, but suddenly the other languages disappeared.

JMc: Thank you very much for your answers to those questions. That's given us an excellent picture of phonetic study in the nineteenth century and up into the beginning of the twentieth century.

MA: Well, thank you, James. It's been a pleasure.

Primary sources

Brücke, Ernst Wilhelm von. 1856. *Grundzüge der Physiologie und Systematik der Sprachlaute für Linguisten und Taubstummenlehrer.* Vienna: Carl Gerold's Sohn.

Bunsen, Christian Karl Josias. 1854. Alphabetical conferences. In *Christianity and mankind: Their beginnings and prospects*, 377–488. London: Longman, Brown, Green.

Helmholtz, Hermann Ludwig Ferdinand von. 1863. *Die Lehre von den Tonempfindungen als physiologische Grundlage für die Theorie der Musik.* Braunschweig: Vieweg.

Helmholtz, Hermann Ludwig Ferdinand von. 1885. *On the sensations of tone, as a physiological basis for the theory of music.* Trans. by Alexander John Ellis. 2nd ed. London: Longmans, Green & Co.

Lepsius, Karl Richard. 1863. *Standard alphabet for reducing unwritten languages and foreign graphic systems to a uniform orthography in European letters.* London: Williams & Norgate.

Müller, Friedrich Max. 1864. *Lectures on the science of language delivered at the Royal Institution of Great Britain in February, March, April and May 1863: Second series.* See pages 103–175 for "The physiological alphabet". London: Longman.

Rousselot, Pierre Jean. 1891. *Les modifications phonétiques du langage, étudiées dans le patois d'une famille de Cellefrouin (Charente).* Paris: H. Welter.

Sievers, Eduard. 1876. *Grundzüge der Phonetik zur Einführung in das Studium der Lautlehre der indogermanischen Sprachen.* Leipzig: Breitkopf und Härtel.

Sweet, Henry. 1877. *A handbook of phonetics.* Oxford: Clarendon Press.

Viëtor, Wilhelm. 1882. *Der Sprachunterricht muss umkehren!* Heilbron: Henninger.

Secondary sources

Ashby, Michael & Marija Tabain. 2020. Fifty years of JIPA. *Journal of the International Phonetic Association* 50(3). 445–448. DOI: 10.1017/S0025100320000298.

Ashby, Michael George. 2016. *Experimental phonetics in Britain, 1890–1940*. Oxford DPhil. Oxford University Research Archive. (Doctoral dissertation).

Kemp, J. Alan. 2006. Phonetic transcription: History. In Keith Brown & Anne H. Anderson (eds.), *Encyclopedia of language and linguistics*, 2nd ed., 396–410. Amsterdam: Elsevier.

Kohler, Klaus. 1981. Three trends in phonetics: The development of phonetics as a discipline in Germany since the nineteenth-century. In Ronald Eaton Asher & Eugénie J. A. Henderson (eds.), *Towards a history of phonetics: In honour of David Abercrombie*, 161–178. Edinburgh: Edinburgh University Press.

Leopold, Joan. 1999. *The Prix Volney, 1a, 1b*. Dordrecht: Kluwer Academic Publishers.

MacMahon, Michael K. C. 1986. The International Phonetic Association: The first 100 years. *Journal of the International Phonetic Association* 16(1). 30–38. DOI: 10.1017/S002510030000308X.

McElvenny, James. 2019. Alternating sounds and the formal franchise in phonology. In *Form and formalism in linguistics*, 35–58. Berlin: Language Science Press.

Chapter 6

Émile Beneveniste

Chloé Laplantine[a] & James McElvenny[b]

[a]University of Paris, CNRS Histoire des théories linguistiques [b]University of Siegen

JMc: In recent interviews, we've been talking about the history of linguistic structuralism in Europe. We've mentioned that it was above all in France where structuralism really took hold. By the middle of the twentieth century, structuralism in France had become something of an official doctrine underpinning the humanities and social sciences. To get a better idea of the career of French structuralism, we're joined today by Chloé Laplantine from the CNRS Laboratory for the History of Linguistic Theories in Paris. She's going to tell us in particular about the life and work of Émile Benveniste, a key figure in French linguistics, who did much to elaborate structuralist thought.

So, Chloé, tell us: Who was Émile Benveniste? How did he become one of the leading French linguists of the twentieth century?

CL: Thank you very much, James, for inviting me to answer your questions. It's a pleasure to talk today with you about Émile Benveniste, who is indeed considered an important linguist of the twentieth century. I'll try today to shed light on his original contributions to reflection on language.

Let's first say a few words about his life and career. Benveniste was born in Aleppo, Syria, in 1902. His parents where teachers for the Alliance israélite internationale. He was sent to Paris in 1913 to pursue rabbinic studies, to become a rabbi, at the Petit séminaire. There, he met Sylvain Lévi, who was filling in for another teacher during the war. Sylvain Lévi – who belonged to the same generation as Ferdinand de Saussure – was an important figure in Oriental studies,

Chloé Laplantine & James McElvenny. 2022. Émile Beneveniste. In James McElvenny (ed.), *Interviews in the history of linguistics: Volume I*, 61–66. Berlin: Language Science Press. DOI: 10.5281/zenodo.7096298 particularly interested in Sanskrit, in the history of Indian religion and culture, teaching Sanskrit language and literature at the Collège de France.

Sylvain Lévi apparently found in Benveniste a promising student, and sent him to the Sorbonne. At the Sorbonne, Benveniste attended the classes of Joseph Vendryès, with whom he studied Celtic linguistics, and under whose direction he wrote his first essay in 1920, "The sigmatic futures and subjunctives in Archaic Latin". Benveniste also attended the classes in comparative grammar given by Antoine Meillet at the Collège de France, as well as frequenting the École des langues orientales, where he studied Sanskrit with Jules Bloch and Vedic with Louis Finot. Rounding things out, he also studied Latin paleography with Émile Chatelain at the École des hautes études.

Benveniste was one of the young and brilliant students who were gathering around Antoine Meillet. Others we should also mention include Louis Renou, Pierre Chantraine, Jerzy Kuryłowicz, and Marie-Louise Sjoestedt. As we can already see, Benveniste's work originated in the French tradition of Oriental studies, comparative grammar, philology, and within the framework of existing institutions like the École des hautes études, the Collège de France, the Société de linguistique de Paris, the Sorbonne and the École des langues orientales.

In 1927, Meillet invited Benveniste, then aged only 25, to replace him at the École des hautes études, and 10 years later, in 1937 he was named to the chair of comparative grammar at the prestigious Collège de France, again replacing Meillet who had died the previous year.

Now that we have seen the institutional background to Benveniste's work, let's go into details. What strikes me the most when looking at the classes Benveniste gave at the Collège de France – when reading their summaries or consulting his manuscripts – is his understanding of the notion of "comparative grammar". We can see that from the beginning, that is to say 1937, he examined general problems in linguistics on the empirical basis of a great variety of languages, which was something quite new at the time. Meillet, teaching comparative grammar before Benveniste, was already looking for data in non-Indo-European language families, but with Benveniste – who was trained as an Indo-Europeanist – we see clearly that linguistics is not only Indo-European linguistics, or even more so that our knowledge about languages can be refined or even renewed in light of non-Indo-European languages.

This might make us think of Franz Boas or Edward Sapir in America. Just to give an example, one of Benveniste's first lectures in 1937 was devoted to the notion of negation; a look at the manuscripts shows us that he was particularly interested in the system of negation in Greek, but also collected quite a bit of information on negation in many different languages – Chinook, Inuit (which back then was usually called "Eskimo"), Khoekhoe (back then called "Hottentot"), Yakut, German, etc. What is more, his research doesn't consist in a collection of facts but leads to the formulation of a general theory of negation. We also see from his notes that, while preparing his class, he was reading Jespersen on negation in English, Jacob van Ginneken's *Principes de linguistique psychologique*, but also Hegel, Henri Bergson on the idea of "nothingness", and Heidegger.

I think this example gives us a good idea of the originality of Benveniste's approach, his openness to the empirical diversity of languages, and the constant tension between this empirical diversity and the formulation of a general linguistic theory. We might quote here a passage from one of his articles, "Coup d'œil sur le développement de la linguistique", published in 1963. He writes: "It is with languages that the linguist deals, and linguistics is primarily the theory of languages. But [...] the infinitely diverse problems of particular languages have in common that, when stated to a certain degree of generality, they always have a bearing on language in general."

I think, in this passage, we can hear something characteristic of Benveniste's approach, which is to consider that knowledge may always be called into question – and this is not a structuralist attitude. This attitude of critical distance appears clearly in the notion of *problème*, which he frequently uses in his writings, and which he chose for the title of his volume of collected papers, *Problèmes de linguistique générale*, published in 1966.

Most of Benveniste's writings are devoted to problems in Indo-European linguistics. But these articles or books, as specialized as they may sometimes look – if you consider their titles – have in common that they are not confined to a purely linguistic analysis. When Benveniste works on the system of tenses in Latin, or on the distinction between nouns for agents and nouns for actions in Indo-European, his analysis of the formal system of the languages brings to light unconscious cultural representations.

We can offer another example: in his article "Two different models of the city", Benveniste compares two ways to conceive of the politics involved in the relation of the citizen to the city. He shows that the Latin *civis* is a term of reciprocity and mutuality – one is the *civis* only of another *civis* – and that the derived term *civitas* is the whole of these relations of reciprocity. The equivalent Greek term, *polis*, is quite different: *polis* is an abstract concept from which the term *polites* is derived, the citizen being then only a part of a preconceived whole.

In the same way, when Benveniste works on the notion of rhythm, or on the notion of eternity, by examining the history of linguistic forms through examples taken from philosophers, historians, or poets, he brings to light conceptions specific to particular societies, like an ethnographer would do, and at the same time unveils an archaeology of our conceptions. This is precisely what he did with his book *Le vocabulaire des institutions indo-européennes*, which can be considered a book of linguistic ethnography, a very different approach from that of ethnologists who would generally consider language as something contained within the society. For Benveniste, language is not contained *within* the society; it is the interpreter of society.

JMc: What were the main contributions of Benveniste to structuralist theory and what impact did his work have on the development of structuralism, both within disciplinary linguistics and more broadly?

CL: We see in many of his articles that Benveniste considers Saussure as a starting point for the study of language – not the only one, of course, but an important starting point – and this for several reasons, among which we can mention the idea that language is a *form*, not a *substance*, that language is never given as a physical object would be, but only exists in one's point of view, and thus the necessity for the linguist to acquire a critical distance and consciousness of his or her own practice. Saussure speaks of the necessity of *showing the linguist what he or she does*.

Benveniste recognizes everywhere the importance of Saussure, but also says that what proves the fertility of a theory lies in the contradictions to which it gives rise. In "La nature du signe linguistique" published in the first issue of *Acta Linguistica* in 1939, he argues, against Saussure, that the relation between the concept and the acoustic image is not *arbitrary* but *necessary*, the idea of arbitrariness being, according to Benveniste, a residue of substantialist conceptions of language. In articles such as "La forme et le sens dans le langage", in 1966, or "Sémiologie de la langue", in 1968, Benveniste invites us to go beyond Saussure and the dimension of the sign, which, according to him, is only one aspect of the problem of language and doesn't do justice to its living reality. He suggests a tension between two dimensions: one that he calls "semiotic" which is the dimension of the *sign*, and involves the faculty of recognition (a sign exists or does not exist); the other dimension is called "semantic", it is the universe of *discourse* and *meaning*, its unity being the *sentence* and the faculty involved being *comprehension*.

Here we find not only something new in comparison with Saussure, but also something that does not match at all with structuralist presuppositions. This point of view on language is totally different as it is now conceived as an activity. Each enunciation is a unique event which vanishes as soon as it is uttered. It is never predictable; the universe of discourse is infinite. Benveniste writes that "[t]o say 'hello' to somebody every day is each time a reinvention", and you'll notice that he chooses a sentence word as an example. You can repeat the same word; it is never the same enunciation.

Another notion that goes with enunciation is that of subjectivity. Benveniste criticizes the reduction of language to an instrument of communication which supposed the separation of language from the human speaker. For Benveniste, the speaker is *in* language, and even more constitutes themselves in and through language as a *subject*. We can quote here a manuscript note: "Language as lived[.] Everything depends on that: in language taken on and lived as a human experience, nothing has the same meaning as with language viewed as a formal system and described from the outside."

In 1967 Benveniste undertook research on the French poet Charles Baudelaire. Maybe it was an answer to Jakobson and Levi-Strauss's structuralist analysis of Baudelaire's poem *Les Chats* published in 1962. When Jakobson and Levi-Strauss take the poem to pieces, analyse it with the tools of structuralist linguistics, nothing remains of the originality of Baudelaire's poem. Their analysis could be repeated indifferently with any poem. What Benveniste tries to do in opposition to this is to show how Baudelaire re-invents language in his poems, how he invents an original experience or vision that he shares with the reader. This research on Baudelaire's language, which was never published, develops an important reflection on meaning. A poem by Baudelaire doesn't work the same way as ordinary language. For Benveniste, Baudelaire creates a *new semiology*, a language that escapes the conventions of discourse.

So I think we've seen that Benveniste's work extends far beyond the framework of structuralist thought. I mentioned earlier his curiosity about linguistic diversity. I could have said a few words about the research he did in 1952 and '53 on the Northwest Coast of America on the Haida, Tlingit, and Gwich'in languages. His curiosity about these languages and cultures was motivated, among other reasons, by an interrogation of *meaning*: he wanted to investigate the ways language signifies and symbolizes. And he had the feeling that linguistics, in particular in America, didn't care about meaning anymore. But for Benveniste, much more than a means of communication, language is a means of living: *Bien avant de servir à communiquer, le langage sert à vivre.*

JMc: That's great. Thank you very much, Chloé, for talking to us today.

CL: Thank you very much, James!

Chloé Laplantine & James McElvenny

Primary sources

Annuaire du Collège de France. 1937–1938. Paris: Ernest Leroux.

Benveniste, Émile. 1937. La négation (manuscript notes). Bibliothèque nationale de France. Département des Manuscrits. Papiers d'orientalistes 33, f°333–484.

Benveniste, Émile. 1966. *Problèmes de linguistique générale.* Paris: Gallimard.

Benveniste, Émile. 1969. *Le vocabulaire des institutions indo-européennes.* Paris: Minuit.

Benveniste, Émile. 1971. *Problems in general linguistics.* Trans. by Mary Elizabeth Meek Gables. Coral Gables: University of Miami Press.

Benveniste, Émile. 1974. *Problèmes de linguistique générale.* 2nd ed. Paris: Gallimard.

Benveniste, Émile. 2011. *Baudelaire.* Chloé Laplantine (ed.). Limoges: Éditions Lambert-Lucas.

Benveniste, Émile. 2012. *Dernières leçons: Collège de France, 1968 et 1969.* Jean-Claude Coquet & Irène Fenoglio (eds.). Paris: École des Hautes Études en Sciences Sociales, Gallimard, Seuil.

Benveniste, Émile. 2015. *Langues, cultures, religions.* Chloé Laplantine & Georges-Jean Pinault (eds.). Limoges: Éditions Lambert-Lucas.

Jakobson, Roman & Claude Lévi-Strauss. 1962. Les "chats" de Baudelaire. *L'homme* 2(1). 5–21.

Jespersen, Otto. 1917. *Negation in English and other languages.* Copenhagen: A. F. Høst Publication.

Secondary sources

Adam, Jean-Michel & Chloé Laplantine (eds.). 2012. *Semen 33, Les notes manuscrites de Benveniste sur la langue de Baudelaire. Besançon : Annales littéraires de l'Université de Franche-Comté.* http://semen.revues.org/9442.

Dessons, Gérard. 2006. *Émile Benveniste. L'invention du discours.* Paris: Éditions In Press.

Laplantine, Chloé. 2011. *Émile Benveniste, l'inconscient et le poème.* Limoges: Éditions Lambert-Lucas.

Laplantine, Chloé. 2019. Questions d'art – terrae incognitae. In Irène Fenoglio & Giuseppe D'Ottavi (eds.), *Emile Benveniste. Un demi siècle après Problèmes de linguistique générale,* 141–151. Paris: Presses de la rue d'Ulm.

Chapter 7

Victoria Lady Welby

H. Walter Schmitz[a] & James McElvenny[b]

[a]University College London [b]University of Siegen

JMc: Today we're joined by Walter Schmitz, Emeritus Professor of Communication Science at the University of Duisburg-Essen. He's going to talk to us about
Victoria Lady Welby, an important and yet perhaps still somewhat underappre-
ciated figure in the history of semiotics. To get us started, could you please tell
us about Victoria Welby's work and the background to it? What were her major
contributions to semiotic thought?

WS: Lady Welby was born in 1837 and died in 1912. She didn't have any formal
education. Instead, she had private lessons, and travelled a lot, especially with
her mother – to the United States, northern Africa, and Syria. Later she became
Maid of Honour to Queen Victoria, in the 1860s, for two years.

After her marriage, she turned to the study of hermeneutics and problems of
interpretation. Her starting point was trying to find arguments against the fun-
damentalist interpretation of the Athanasian creed and other theological and biblical texts. Afterwards, she studied philosophy and natural sciences. Everywhere
she found puzzling terminology, but she found nobody cared for meaning, for
meaning of terminology, for meaning of ordinary words, and so she embarked
on a critique of terminology and ordinary language, and she found that the language that many scholars were using was not in agreement with the results of
the sciences. Through her work, she introduced the study of meaning as a topic
into British philosophy, psychology, and even linguistics. In 1896, she published
her first article in the philosophical journal *Mind* on sense, meaning and interpretation.

H. Walter Schmitz & James McElvenny. 2022. Victoria Lady Welby. In
James McElvenny (ed.), *Interviews in the history of linguistics: Volume I*, 67–74.
Berlin: Language Science Press. DOI: 10.5281/zenodo.7096300

Lady Welby's contribution to semiotics was quite different from others at the time. Unlike C. S. Peirce, she did not proceed from definitions of signs and their features in order to investigate the relations into which signs with certain features can enter. Rather, she started from the other side, so to speak, and concentrated on the problem of meaning; that is, on questions of interpretation and the communicative use of signs. This is the essential merit of her contribution.

JMc: You say that Welby started with Bible interpretation, or hermeneutics. This task of Bible interpretation also played a major role in German intellectual life in the nineteenth century, and in the study of meaning in the nineteenth century in Germany. Why do you think Lady Welby turned to hermeneutics? Was it because she was particularly religious, or did it have more to do with the fact that this was one of the few intellectual outlets that was available to her because she couldn't get a formal education?

WS: I think the roots were in practical problems. She was a mother and had to educate her children, and as a very independent person – mentally, financially, and in every respect independent – she asked herself: How can I educate my children in religious questions? She couldn't find a suitable answer in the ecclesiastical books available to her, so she started to study biblical texts and ask herself: How should I understand these texts? Do I need a new interpretation, a contemporary interpretation?

Lady Welby couldn't read German or French, but only English, so she concentrated on what she could find written in English, especially in ecclesiastical books. But at that time it was not permitted for women to have such interests. That was a serious problem for her. Indeed, when she published her first book in 1881 – with a second edition in 1883 – many of her relatives claimed to find it offensive. She had to defend herself against the aggression of church people and even those in her own circle of acquaintances.

JMc: Let's briefly expand on this problem of her not being able to get a formal education. As you mentioned, she was born in 1837, and as far as I'm aware, the first English university that allowed women to attend classes was the University of London in 1868, so she would have already been an adult by that stage. Even then, the female students at the University of London weren't allowed to take degrees, so they were still second-class citizens in the university world.

Lady Welby is in fact the first woman to have appeared in our podcast series so far, right at the end of the nineteenth century. It's nice that we've finally been able to find a woman scholar who was able to fight against all of the restrictions that were put on her gender in this period, but on the other hand, it's still a story of privilege, isn't it? She was a member of the high aristocracy, she was financially independent, she was the Maid of Honour to Queen Victoria – in fact, she was named after Queen Victoria, who was her godmother.

WS: Yes, she knew how to use her privilege in order to get on with her studies. She invited other scholars to come to her manor in Lincolnshire and held discussions with them. Her guests included such figures as the psychologist G. F. Stout, or philosophers like Ferderik Canning Scott Schiller, or mathematicians and philosophers like Bertrand Russell. She sent them her essays and discussed the essays with them. Through her correspondence, she got feedback on her writings and eventually arrived at publishable versions. So she collaborated with others and used her privilege in order to overcome lack of knowledge, lack of experience. Even in writing scientific texts, she had assistants who helped her to write the books.

JMc: On a purely political level, I believe she could not be considered a feminist. She was an opponent of the suffragettes, for example – she didn't support women's suffrage.

WS: In political questions, I think that's not the only argument to call her very conservative. Especially in the discussions with Frederik van Eeden – a Dutch poet and psychiatrist she corresponded with and knew very well – she was a vocal supporter of the British Empire in the Boer War against the Dutch colonists in South Africa. In those questions, she was a conservative, a member of her class.

But in her scholarship, she was very progressive. She brought the topic of meaning into British philosophy. Ogden and Richards' later work on meaning, and even Bertrand Russell's interest in the topic all started with Lady Welby's work. On the folder in which he kept his correspondence with Lady Welby, Russell wrote: "From Lady Welby, who turned my attention to linguistic questions." I think at that time, in 1905, for example, when Russell wrote about "On denoting", he didn't understand her very well. She was far in advance of him, and she argued against Russell in the same way as P. F. Strawson did many years later. So in this respect she was progressive, but in political respects, she was a conservative, yes.

JMc: But didn't Russell write in some of his correspondence that he refused the invitation to go to Welby's house because he would have had to be honest with her, and he thinks that it's a shame that everyone is encouraging her?

WS: I think at that time Russell didn't think very highly of Lady Welby. But later on, he recognized that she showed the right way. Even in 1920, when there was a symposium organized on the meaning of meaning, Russell participated in that symposium, but he wrote a paper that took a very behaviouristic approach to meaning, while Ferdinand Canning Scott Schiller, the philosopher, was a defender of Lady Welby's approach. Russell needed more time to learn than others.

JMc: Do you think Russell ever did learn? He was still fighting ordinary language philosophers in the 1950s and '60s.

WS: I'd say even when he wrote, "She called attention to linguistic questions", it was a kind of misunderstanding. Lady Welby wasn't interested in linguistic questions; she was interested in ways of interpreting signs, and that's a more general question than a linguistic one. For her, the word outside of use has a verbal meaning, but it doesn't have sense; it has no meaning. Her interest was in the meaning of signs and not in words or in a systematic description of language.

JMc: OK, so this is a keyword that brings us to the heart of her doctrines, namely this trichotomy that she set up between sense, meaning and significance. Could you explain what that means?

WS: Let's begin with sense. Lady Welby sought a very broad concept of sense, and it was a kind of organismic concept. "Sense", in its broadest sense, is for Lady Welby the suitable term for that which constitutes the value of experience in this life on this planet. The value of the experience which is had consists of the sort of organic reaction (touch, smell, taste, hearing or sight) to a stimulus which is at the same time an interpretation or translation of the stimulus influenced by the physiology of human senses (so Fritz Mauthner speaks quite correctly of our *Zufallssinne* "chance senses").

But words or utterances have sense or acquire sense through the interpretation of the hearer or reader. The first reaction is the sense of the utterance, while meaning is the intention which is combined with the utterance, so the interpreter has to find out the difference between sense and meaning.

The sense is what we get almost immediately, but in order to get to the meaning of an utterance, we have to draw conclusions. For example, somebody might ask me, "Where is Peter?" and I answer, "Yesterday, I saw a yellow Porsche in front of house number seven." The sense of my utterance might be, "Yesterday, there was such and such an event which I experienced", but the meaning of my utterance is quite different: "Peter was in that house."

Now we come to significance. The significance is a consequence of or an implication of the utterance or even an event, even experience. So it might be that there is a woman who lives in house number seven, and the person who asked me where Peter is was perhaps Peter's wife. She may be afraid that Peter went to another woman. So the consequence or the implication of my utterance might be of very great importance to her. Significance is the third meaning events or utterances or words may have.

JMc: In 1909, C. S. Peirce wrote to Welby in a letter that his own tripartition of immediate interpretant, dynamical interpretant, and final interpretant, "nearly coincides with your sense, meaning and significance". You mentioned at the beginning of the interview the two different directions that Peirce and Welby approach the problems of semiotics from, but Peirce seems to have thought himself that his own views and Welby's were very close.

WS: Peirce did indeed write that to Lady Welby, and I think there are some similarities between their views, but they aren't identical. Immediate interpretant, for instance, has some similarities with sense but it's not quite identical, and the dynamical interpretant is even less similar to Lady Welby's meaning. Perhaps final interpretant and significance might be more similar than even Peirce thought, but Peirce's and Welby's respective approaches were so different that we couldn't expect that their terms should be used to name the same concepts.

The differences shouldn't be overlooked. I think for Peirce, it was important to have somebody to discuss semiotic questions with, somebody to explain his ideas on semiotics to, so that at times he overlooked the differences. She did much the same thing. Peirce wasn't interested in communication and interpretation. He was interested in the development of a general semiotic system, and he left it as an empirical question to find out where and how these classes of signs were realized in real events. That's a very different approach, and it has to get to very different aims.

JMc: So could you tell us then a bit about what happened to Lady Welby's legacy, to her work in later generations? There was the Dutch Significs movement, as it's known, a group of scholars in the Netherlands who took Lady

Welby's work as an inspiration and continued in that line, but I think it's probably fair to say that since that time there hasn't been much interest in her work, except a resurgence, say, since the 1980s onwards with semioticians looking at the history of semiotics. But these semioticians weren't deploying her theories actively to make new analyses, but rather just trying to uncover the past.

WS: That's right. Even the Signific movement in the Netherlands didn't go the same way as Lady Welby. She was just a source of inspiration, and the Dutch scholars, especially Gerrit Mannoury, developed a kind of psychological communication theory. What happened to Lady Welby's ideas was a kind of unacknowledged, clandestine continuation. If you look at the book by Ogden and Richards, *The meaning of meaning*, there you find a lot of elements of Lady Welby's work. Even if Ogden and Richards tried to hide it, they were standing on Lady Welby's shoulders.

JMc: And of course, Ogden was one of Lady Welby's assistants.

WS: Yes, yes. And Ogden copied, for example, the important letters from Peirce to Welby, and printed them in the appendix of *The meaning of meaning*. The personal idealism of Ferdinand Canning Scott Schiller was also in some respects influenced by Lady Welby's theory. Even in the novels of H. G. Wells, you can find traces of Lady Welby. Especially the late novel *The shape of things to come* gets to Ogden and Richards and to Lady Welby, and he knows very well the connection between Welby and Ogden, for example. Another more or less clandestine trace is in General Semantics. Korzybski and Hayakawa were very familiar with the writings of Lady Welby.

Lady Welby was important in her day, but in a certain respect it was good to go beyond the initial inspiration she provided. But semiotics has never again found a way to study the use of signs in communication. Semioticians since Lady Welby's time have all focused exclusively on creating a taxonomy of signs, as Peirce and Saussure did, but the question of how signs are used in communication is largely neglected in semiotics today. Perhaps it has wandered into conversational analysis, but it has left semiotics.

JMc: Thank you very much for this interview.

WS: Thank you for your interest in the topic.

Primary sources

Hayakawa, Samuel Ichiyé. 1939. *Language in thought and action*. New York: Harcourt, Brace & Co.

Ogden, Charles K. & Ivor A. Richards. 1949 [1923]. *The meaning of meaning: A study of the influence of language upon thought and the science of symbolism*. London: Routledge.

Russell, Bertrand. 1905. On denoting. *Mind* 14(4). 479–493.

Schiller, Ferdinand Canning Scott, Bertrand Russell & Harold Henry Joachim. 1920. The meaning of "meaning": a symposium. *Mind* 29(116). 385–414.

Strawson, Peter F. 1950. On referring. *Mind* 59(235). 320–344.

Welby, Victoria Lady. 1883 [1881]. *Links and clues*. London: Macmillan & Co.

Welby, Victoria Lady. 1897. *Grains of sense*. London: J. M. Dent & Co.

Welby, Victoria Lady. 1983 [1903]. *What is meaning?* Amsterdam: John Benjamins.

Welby, Victoria Lady. 1985 [1893]. Meaning and metaphor. In H. Walter Schmitz (ed.), *Significs and language: The articulate form of our expressive and interpretative resources*, 510–525. Reproduced with original pagination (original in *The Monist* 3(4). 510–525).

Welby, Victoria Lady. 1985 [1896]. Sense, meaning and interpretation. In H. Walter Schmitz (ed.), *Significs and language: The articulate form of our expressive and interpretative resources*. Reproduced with original pagination (original in two parts in *Mind* 5(17). 24–37 and 5(18). 186–202).

Welby, Victoria Lady. 1985 [1911]. *Significs and language: The articulate form of our expressive and interpretative resources*. H. Walter Schmitz (ed.). Amsterdam: Benjamins.

Welby, Victoria Lady, George Frederick Stout & James Mark Baldwin. 1902. Significs. In J.M. Baldwin (ed.), *Dictionary of philosophy and psychology in three volumes*, vol. 2, 529. New York: Macmillan.

Wells, H. G. 1933. *The shape of things to come*. London: Hutchison.

Secondary sources

Heijerman, Erik & H. Walter Schmitz (eds.). 1991. *Significs, mathematics and semiotics: The signific movement in the Netherlands: Proceedings of the international conference Bonn*. Münster: Nodus Publikationen.

McElvenny, James. 2014. Ogden and Richards' *The Meaning of Meaning* and early analytic philosophy. *Language Sciences* 41. 212–221.

McElvenny, James. 2018. *Language and meaning in the age of modernism: C. K. Ogden and his contemporaries.* Edinburgh: Edinburgh University Press.

Nuessel, Frank, Vincent Colapietro & Susan Petrilli (eds.). 2013. *Semiotica (Special Issue): On and beyond Significs: Centennial issue for Victoria Lady Welby (1837–1912).* Vol. 196(1/4).

Petrilli, Susan P. 2009. *Signifying and understanding: Reading the works of Victoria Welby and the Signific movement.* Berlin: De Gruyter.

Petrilli, Susan P. 2015. *Victoria Lady Welby and the science of signs: Significs, semiotics, philosophy of language.* New Brunswick: Transaction.

Schmitz, H. Walter. 1985. Tönnies' Zeichentheorie zwischen Signifik und Wiener Kreis. *Zeitschrift für Soziologie* 14(5). 373–385.

Schmitz, H. Walter. 1990a. *De Hollandse Significa: Een reconstructie van de geschiedenis van 1892 tot 1926.* Vertaling: Jacques van Nieuwstadt.

Schmitz, H. Walter (ed.). 1990b. *Essays on Significs: Papers presented on the occasion of the 150th anniversary of the birth of Victoria Lady Welby (1837–1912).* Amsterdam: John Benjamins.

Schmitz, H. Walter. 1993. Lady Welby on sign and meaning, context and interpretation. *Kodikas/Code* 16(1). 19–28.

Schmitz, H. Walter. 1995. Anmerkungen zum Welby-Russell-Briefwechsel. In Klaus D. Dutz & Kjell-Åke Forsgren (eds.), *History and rationality. The Skövde papers in the historiography of linguistics*, 293–305. Münster: Nodus Publikationen.

Schmitz, H. Walter. 1998. Die Signifik. In Roland Posner, Klaus Robering & Thomas A. Sebeok (eds.), *Semiotik. Semiotics. Ein Handbuch zu den zeichentheoretischen Grundlagen von Natur und Kultur. A Handbook on the sign-theoretic foundations of nature and culture*, vol. 2, 2112–2117. Berlin/New York: Walter de Gruyter.

Schmitz, H. Walter. 2009. Welby, Victoria Lady. In Harro Stammerjohann (ed.), *Lexicon grammaticorum: A bio-bibliographical companion to the history of linguistics*, 2nd ed., vol. II, L–Z, 1627–1628. Tübingen: Niemeyer.

Schmitz, H. Walter. 2011. Archiv und Anthologie der Signifik – in einem einzigen Band? *Beiträge zur Geschichte der Sprachwissenschaft* 21(1). 127–152.

Schmitz, H. Walter. 2014. "It is confusion and misunderstanding that we must first attack or we must fail hopelessly in the long run." Taking stock of the published correspondence of Victoria Lady Welby. *Kodikas/Code* 36(3/4). 203–226.

Chapter 8

John Rupert Firth, Bronisław Malinowski, and the London School

Jacqueline Léon[a] & James McElvenny[b]

[a]University of Paris, CNRS Histoire des theories linguistiques [b]University of Siegen

JMc: Today we explore the work of the London School of linguistics, whose institutional figurehead was John Rupert Firth, and which had many links outside disciplinary linguistics, perhaps most notably to the ethnographic work of Bronisław Malinowski. To take us through this topic, we're joined by Jacqueline Léon, from the CNRS Laboratory for the History of Linguistic Theories in Paris.

A key concept for both Firth and Malinowski was the "context of situation". You've argued, Jacqueline, that this concept represents a kind of anticipation of ideas that were later reinvented or rediscovered under the rubrics of ethnography of communication and conversation analysis. What exactly are the common points between Firthian linguistics and these later approaches? And are there direct historical connections between them or were the later ideas developed independently?

JL: One can say that there is a direct connection between Firth and Malinowski's ideas and ethnography of communication, since its pioneers, Dell Hymes and John Gumperz, consider Malinowski and Firth among the notable sources of the field. In his introductory book to ethnography of communication, *Language in Culture and Society*, published in 1964, Hymes reproduces the second part of Firth's text "The technique of semantics" of 1935 under the title of "Sociological linguistics". Remember that, in that text, Firth starts to elaborate the notion of

Jacqueline Léon & James McElvenny. 2022. John Rupert Firth, Bronisław Malinowski, and the London School. In James McElvenny (ed.), *Interviews in the history of linguistics: Volume I*, 75–82. Berlin: Language Science Press. DOI: 10.5281/zenodo.7096302

context of situation in the wake of Malinowski. In the same book, Hymes also reproduces a text by Malinowski of 1937 called "The Dilemma of Contemporary Linguistics".

Later, in their introductory book *Directions in Sociolinguistics, The Ethnography of Communication*, published in 1972, Gumperz and Hymes underline what dialectology and variation studies owe to Firth, in particular with the notions of context of situation, speech community, and verbal repertories, and how their notion of frame comes from the functional categories of the context of situation. They also claim their affiliation to Firth's article "Personality and language in society", published in 1950.

As for conversation analysis, the connection is less direct: Sacks and Schegloff, the pioneers of conversation analysis, never quote Firth or Malinowski. However, they both refer to Hymes, and Sacks is one of the authors of *Directions in Sociolinguistics*, edited by Gumperz and Hymes in 1972, so that one can claim that they were acquainted with Firth's and Malinowski's writings.

Now, let's look into this in more detail, specifically Malinowski's and Firth's context of situation and their conception of language as a mode of action. In *Coral gardens and their magic*, Malinowski's context of situation includes not only linguistic context but also gestures, looks, facial expressions and perceptual context. More broadly, context of situation is identified with the cultural context comprising all the people participating in the activity, as well as the physical and social environment. In other words, context of situation is the nonverbal matrix of the speech event. Malinowski gives words the power to act, that is to say, long before Austin's *How to do things with words* (delivered as lectures in 1955 and published 1962). Malinowski says, "Words in their first and essential sense do, act, produce and realize."

As for Firth, as early as 1935, in "The technique of semantics", he emphasizes the importance of conversation for the study of language. I quote: "Conversation is much more of a roughly prescribed ritual than most people think. Once someone speaks to you, you are in a relatively determined context and you are not free just to say what you please. [...] Neither linguists nor psychologists have begun the study of conversation; but it is here that we shall find the key to a better understanding of what language really is and how it works."

In this text, Firth presents a linguistic treatment of the context of situation. He groups the contexts by type of use, genres, and what was later called "register", divided into the dimensions: (a) common, colloquial, slang, literary, technical, scientific, conversational, dialectal; (b) speaking, hearing, writing, reading; (c) familiar, colloquial, and more formal speech; (d) the languages of the schools, the law, the church, and specialized forms of speech. These categories become the basis of his notion of "restricted languages", which he developed from 1945.

To these types of monological uses, Firth adds those created by the interactions between several people where the function of phatic communion identified by Malinowski is at work. The examples he gives are acts of ordinary conversation, such as addresses, greetings, mutual recognition, etc., or belong to institutions like the church, the tribunal, administration, where words are deeds. I quote Firth again: "In more detail we may notice such common situations as:

"(a) Address: 'Simpson!' 'Look here, Jones', 'My dear boy', 'Now, my man', 'Excuse me, madam'.

"(b) Greetings, farewells, or mutual recognition of status and relationship on contact, adjustment of relations after contact, breaking off relations, renewal of relations, change of relations.

"(c) Situations in which words, often conventionally fixed by law or custom, serve to bind people to a line of action or to free them from certain customary duties in order to impose others. In Churches, Law Courts, Offices, such situations are commonplace."

However, the notion of situation, and the classification of these situations, seemed to him insufficient to account for language as action. Instead, he proposes linguistic functions reduced to linguistic expressions: he speaks of the languages of agreement, disagreement, encouragement, approval, condemnation; the action of wishing, blessing, cursing, boasting; the language of challenge, flattery, seduction, compliments, blame, propaganda and persuasion.

Here we can recognize the first objects studied by the first conversation analysts in their research on talk-in-interaction, that is, greetings, compliments, agreement and disagreement, etc. In *The Tongues of Men*, published in 1937, two years after "The technique of semantics", appeared what was later formalized as turn-taking organization and action sequences by the conversation analysts. Firth evokes the mutual expectations aroused in the interlocutors as well as the limited range of possibilities of responses to a given turn.

As for the notions relating to language variation, which would prove to be very important for ethnographers of communication, they were developed by Firth from 1950. Firth already developed the notion of "specialized languages" in his efforts to teach Japanese to British air force officers during the Second World War. These were subsets of the full language confined to certain domains; that is, the vocabulary, grammar and other constructions one would need to communicate in a specific situation. A few years later, this concept of specialized languages became restricted languages. For Firth, even restricted languages are affected by variation and context. Even in the restricted languages of weather or mathematics, which can nevertheless be regarded as extremely constrained, there are dramatic variations according to the cultures in which they are embedded and to the climates in which they are used.

In Firth's last paper, published in 1959, we come across the idea of repertory, according to which each person is in command of a varied repertory of language roles, of a constellation of restricted languages. The notion of repertory was developed by ethnographers of communication as crucial for the study of variation.

With this final paper, where restricted languages refer to speakers' individual repertories, we could say that Firth gave the outline of the notion of register later developed by his followers, especially Michael Halliday, Angus McIntosh and Paul Strevens in their book *The Linguistic Sciences and Language Teaching*, published in 1964. At first, they worked out the notion of register to address the issue of language variety in connection with foreign language teaching. Linguistic variety should be studied through two distinct notions, dialect and register, to account for linguistic events (Firth's term to designate the linguistic activity of people in situations).

They oppose dialect (that is, variety according to user: varieties in the sense that each speaker uses one variety and uses it all the time) to register (that is, variety according to use: in the sense that each speaker has a range of varieties and chooses between them at different times). The category of "register" refers to the type of language selected by a speaker as appropriate to different types of situations. Within this framework, restricted languages are referred to as specific, constrained types of registers which, I quote, "employ only a limited number of formal items and patterns."

It should be added that the authors – that is, Halliday et al. – refer to Ferguson and Gumperz's work on *Linguistic diversity in South Asia*, Weinreich's *Languages in contact* and Quirk's *Use of English*, in addition to Firth's work, so that it should be said that registers had not been the direct successors of restricted languages. They have been established on Firthian views already revisited by Hymes and Gumperz, and then by Halliday and his colleagues.

In conclusion, one can claim that Firth's context of situation, linguistic events, restricted languages, and repertories raised crucial issues for early sociolinguistics.

JMc: So Firthian linguistics would seem to have a very pragmatic and applied character. What's the relationship of Firthian theory to what the British call "applied linguistics"? And how does this relate to the Firthian notion of "restricted languages", which you just mentioned in your answer to the previous question?

JL: To answer this question, I must recall that there is a specific tradition of applied linguistics coming from British empiricism, which, since the nineteenth century, has rested on the articulation between theory, practice and applications based on technological innovations. Firth played an important role in the development of practical and applied linguistics, which became institutionalized only after his death, in the 1950–1960s, with two pioneering trends, in the US and in Britain. Michael Halliday, one of his most famous pupils, was one of the founders of the AILA, Association Internationale de Linguistique Appliquée, in 1964, and of BAAL, the British Association for Applied Linguistics, in 1967.

Henry Sweet was probably the nineteenth-century linguist who best exemplified the establishment of close links between linguistic theory and its application. Firth was a big admirer of Sweet (in particular, he mentions having learned his shorthand method at 14) and is in line with Sweet's "living philology" in several ways: the priority given to phonetics in the description of languages, the attention paid to text and phonetics, the absence of distinction between practical grammar and theoretical grammar, the important place of descriptive grammar, and finally the involvement in language teaching.

In this last area, Sweet advocated the use of texts written in a simple and direct style, containing only frequent words, instead of learning lists of isolated words or sentences off by heart, which was the usual way of teaching languages in his time. These texts – which he called "connected coherent texts" – recall the restricted languages that Firth would recommend later for language teaching and also for all kinds of applications, such as translation and the study of collocations.

Firth developed restricted language in 1956 – in his article entitled "Descriptive linguistics and the study of English" – even if the idea of specialized language appeared as early as 1950. Firth's major concern at the time was to set up the crucial status of descriptive linguistics, against Saussurian and Neo-Bloomfieldian structural linguistics. Restricted languages were a way to question the monosystemic view of language shared by European structuralists (especially Meillet's view of language as a one-system whole *où tout se tient*), and to criticize pointless discussions on metalanguage. Restricted languages are at the core of his conception of descriptive linguistics, where practical applications are guided by theory. Firth developed restricted languages according to three levels, "language under description", "language of description", "language of translation", each of them determining a step in the description process.

The language under description is the raw material observed, transcribed in the form of "text" located contextually. From a methodological point of view, restricted languages under description should be authentic texts – that is, written texts or the transcription of the raw empirical material. They may be materialized in a single text, such as Magna Carta in Medieval Latin, or the American Declaration of Independence. The language of description corresponds to linguistic terminology and transcription systems – we must know that Firth rejected the concept of metalanguage.

Finally, the translation language includes the source and target languages, and the definition languages of dictionaries and grammars. Firth insists that restricted languages are more suited than general language to carrying out practical purposes, such as teaching languages, translating, or building dictionaries, and to study collocations, a major topic in his later work. Likewise, defined as limited types of a major language, for example subsets of English, contextually situated, they are the privileged object of descriptive linguistics. The task of descriptive linguistics, he said, is not to study the language as a whole, but to study restricted, more manageable languages, which should have their own grammar and dictionary, which he called micro-grammar and micro-glossary.

Firth uses the phrase "the restricted language of X" in order to address the different types of restricted languages: the restricted language of science, technology, sport, defence, industry, aviation, military services, commerce, law and civil administration, politics, literature, etc.

Firth died in 1960, the year of decolonization in Africa, also called "the year of Africa". His last two texts are posthumous speeches at two congresses, organized respectively by the British Council and the Commonwealth on the teaching of English as a foreign language and as a second language in the former colonies. The research on restricted languages initiated by Firth is a central theme addressed in these lectures, under the title "English for special purposes", and it is the Neo-Firthians, as his followers are sometimes called, including Michael Halliday, who took up these questions.

JMc: Thank you very much for your very detailed answers to these questions.

JL: Thank you.

Primary sources

Austin, John L. 1962. *How to do things with words.* Oxford: Oxford University Press.

Biber, Douglas. 1988. *Variation across speech and writing.* Cambridge: Cambridge University Press.

Brown, Keith & Vivien Law (eds.). 2002. *Linguistics in Britain: Personal histories.* Oxford: Publications of the Philological Society.

Firth, John Rupert. 1930. *Speech.* London: Benn's Sixpenny Library.

Firth, John Rupert. 1957 [1935]. The technique of semantics. In *Papers in linguistics (1934–1951)*, 7–33. Oxford: Oxford University Press.

Firth, John Rupert. 1957 [1950]. Personality and language in society. In *Papers in linguistics (1934–1951)*, 177–189. Oxford: Oxford University Press.

Firth, John Rupert. 1957 [1951]. General linguistics and descriptive grammar. In *Papers in linguistics (1934–1951)*, 216–228. Oxford: Oxford University Press.

Firth, John Rupert. 1960. *Conference on university training and research in the use of English as a second / foreign language.* [Posthumous manuscript 1]. British Council, 15–17 December 1960. J. R. Firth collection, SOAS, London, PP MS 75, box 2.

Firth, John Rupert. 1961. *Commonwealth conference of the teaching of English as a second language.* [Posthumous manuscript 2]. Makerere, Uganda, January 1961. J. R. Firth collection, SOAS, London, Personal File. Makerere, Uganda.

Firth, John Rupert. 1968 [1956]. Descriptive linguistics and the study of English. In Frank R. Palmer (ed.), *Selected papers of J. R. Firth (1952–59)*, 96–113. Bloomington: Indiana University Press.

Firth, John Rupert. 1968 [1957]. Ethnographic analysis and language with reference to Malinowski's views. In Frank R. Palmer (ed.), *Selected papers of J. R. Firth (1952–59)*, 137–167. London & Bloomington: Indiana University Press.

Firth, John Rupert. 1968 [1959]. The treatment of language in general linguistics. In Frank R. Palmer (ed.), *Selected papers of J. R. Firth (1952–59)*, 206–209. London & Bloomington: Indiana University Press.

Firth, John Rupert. 1970 [1937]. *The tongues of men.* Oxford: Oxford University Press.

Gumperz, John Joseph & Dell Hymes. 1972. *Directions in sociolinguistics, the ethnography of communication.* New York: Holt Rinehart & Winston.

Halliday, Michael A. K., Angus McIntosh & Paul Strevens. 1964. *The linguistic sciences and language teaching.* London: Longman.

Halliday, Michael A.K. 1966. General linguistics and its application to language teaching. In Michael A. K. Halliday & Angus McIntosh (eds.), *Patterns of language: Papers in general, descriptive and applied linguistics*, 1–41. London: Longman.

Hymes, Dell. 1964. *Language in culture and society. A reader in linguistics and anthropology.* New York: Harper & Row.

Malinowski, Bronislaw. 1923. The problem of meaning in primitive languages. In *The meaning of meaning*, by C. K. Ogden and I. A. Richards, 296–337. London: Routledge & Kegan Paul.

Malinowski, Bronislaw. 1935. *Coral gardens and their magic. The language of magic and gardening.* Vol. II. London: Allen & Unwin.

Malinowski, Bronislaw. 1937. The dilemma of contemporary linguistics. Review of *Infant speech: a study of the beginnings of language*, by M. M. Lewis. *Nature* 140. 172–173.

Sweet, Henry. 1891. *The practical study of languages: A guide for teachers and learners.* Reprinted in 1964 by R. Mackin. Oxford: Oxford University Press.

Sweet, Henry. 1891–1898. *A new English grammar: Logical and historical.* Oxford: Clarendon Press.

Secondary sources

Howatt, Anthony Philip Reid. 1984. *History of English language teaching.* Oxford: Oxford University Press.

Léon, Jacqueline. 2007. From linguistic events and restricted languages to registers. Firthian legacy and corpus linguistics. *The Bulletin of the Henry Sweet Society for the History of Linguistic Ideas* 49. 5–26.

Léon, Jacqueline. 2008. Empirical traditions of computer-based methods. Firth's restricted languages and Harris' sublanguages. *Beiträge zur Geschichte der Sprachwissenschaft* 18(2). 259–274.

Léon, Jacqueline. 2011. De la linguistique descriptive à la linguistique appliquée dans la tradition britannique. Sweet, Firth et Halliday. *Histoire Epistémologie Langage* 33(1). 69–81.

Léon, Jacqueline. 2019. Les sources britanniques de l'ethnographie de la communication et de l'analyse de conversation. Bronislaw Malinowski et John Rupert Firth. *Linha d'Agua* 32(1). 23–38.

Mitchell, Terence Frederick. 1975. *Principles of Firthian linguistics.* London: Longman.

Palmer, Frank R. 1994. Firth and the London School. In Ronald Asher (ed.), *The encyclopedia of language and linguistics*, 1257–1260. Oxford: Pergamon Press.

Rebori, Victoria. 2002. The legacy of J. R. Firth. A report on recent research. *Historiographia Linguistica* 29(1). 165–190.

Stubbs, Michael. 1992. Institutional linguistics: Language and institutions, linguistics and sociology. In Martin Pütz (ed.), *Thirty years of linguistic evolution*, 189–21. Amsterdam: Benjamins.

Chapter 9

Linguistics under National Socialism

Christopher Hutton[a] & James McElvenny[b]
[a]University of Hong Kong [b]University of Siegen

JMc: In the most recent podcast episodes, which have focused on Central Europe in the first half of the twentieth century, we've met a number of figures who were forced into exile by the rise of fascism. In this episode, we turn our attention to those who stayed behind and found a place for themselves and their scholarship under the new regimes. We also take a moment to consider the parallels between this period and today. To guide us through these topics, we're joined by Christopher Hutton, Professor of English Linguistics at the University of Hong Kong.

So, Chris, you've written extensively on the place of language study and anthropology in the so-called Third Reich. Your publications on this topic include the 1999 book *Linguistics in the Third Reich* and the 2005 *Race in the Third Reich*. Can you tell us what the main themes of Nazi language study were? How did these themes differ from language study in the democratic countries of the time?

CH: I think you have to start in the 1920s and '30s. Remember that Germany is really the centre of linguistics internationally at that time. So German linguistics was influential around the world, but it had some peculiarities that were not adopted internationally. One of these is the centrality of the concept of *Volk*. This is very different from, say, French or Anglo-American linguistics. And then you have these ideas about mother tongue and discussions of bilingualism, language islands, *Sprachinselforschung*.

Christopher Hutton & James McElvenny. 2022. Linguistics under National Socialism. In James McElvenny (ed.), *Interviews in the history of linguistics: Volume I*, 83–90. Berlin: Language Science Press. DOI: 10.5281/zenodo.7096304

I think there is a contrast with what's going on in France, and in the UK, and the US. Of course, you do have in the US the Boasian tradition – Humboldt, Boas – but it's focused mainly on indigenous cultures of North America, so it has this kind of niche, and in there, it's a sort of rescue operation in some ways, and in some ways politically liberal. Boas himself counts as a liberal, although there is a more complicated story there, actually.

If you think of Saussure's *langue*, a concept – whatever you make of it – which is very free of some of the ideology that sticks to the German concepts of *Volk* and language community and so on, it seems almost Cartesian in its abstractness, and I think that is very significant. Saussure does have a reception in Germany, and there is structural linguistics, but the idea tends to be that, well, the conceptual structure of the language should have some basis in history, tradition, and so on. So German linguistics is very different from Saussurean structuralism, which, if you take it puristically, is entirely synchronic. There is no real narrative you can make of the history of a language, in a sort of ideological "The story of language X".

I think there is a kind of continental sensibility because of the effect of World War I on state boundaries in Europe, and there is a level of insecurity and uncertainty which doesn't apply in the US and the UK, which really makes a big difference. Because German linguistics falls largely under *Germanistik*, which was an extremely conservative discipline, the people in *Germanistik* on the whole were on the right. They didn't necessarily become true Nazis, but they were certainly on the *völkisch* side, as opposed to, say, sociology in Germany.

JMc: Can I just ask about what you said about Boas, that there's a connection there with the German tradition but that Boas' work was focused on American indigenous languages? Do you think that there's still a connection there, though, with how the German nationalists in Nazi Germany conceived of themselves? Because if you go back into the nineteenth century, there's a lot of sympathy, especially in German pop culture, with the plight of indigenous people in America – if you think of the novels of Karl May, for example. There's also this fascination of the part of German scholars with things like Tacitus's descriptions of the *Germanen* as an indigenous people on the edge of civilization.

CH: I think it's a very good point. Maybe you can look at it this way. There's hostility to the Anglo-American model of the state, as well as to the French model. These are seen as assimilatory and lacking a kind of organic basis: they're capitalist and based in law, in some kind of Common Law, which is an individualistic system and promotes, in a way, social movement and mobility, and also sees property as a resource to be exploited.

Although Boas, being Jewish, and also politically liberal, ends up attacking the Nazis, there are parallels there, and you could put it under hostility to modernity, in a way. Sapir maintains some of the same spirit: the ideal of the Native American fishing in that tranquil way, free of the pressures of the modern industrialized world, the timetable, and so on. It's an attractive image to everybody, but I think this form of Romantic primitivism – or whatever you want to call it – was very powerful in Germany.

And it also spills over into Celtic studies, and the affinity to Celtic music, culture, again, in opposition to this hostile Common Law English state, the colonial settler state which then threatens to obliterate diversity. It's true that Common Law gobbles up diversity. Look at Australia and the *terra nullius* doctrine. Once you're inside the Common Law it may protect you, but if you're faced with it coming at you, it's actually really brutal. They had a point, I think.

JMc: So on this point of Celtic studies, one of the major areas of applied linguistics that thrived under the National Socialist regime – because it aligned very well with the regime's interests – was the issue of minority language rights. This was very prominent in Celtic studies, as you mentioned.

So, first of all, in *Germanistik*, there was the issue of *Auslandsdeutsche* – that is, German speakers who were living outside the political boundaries of Germany, predominantly in Eastern Europe, but also in migrant communities in North America. But the issue of minority language rights was also deployed against the enemies of Nazi Germany – and this is where Celtic studies comes in – in alleged solidarity with oppressed ethnic groups such as the Bretons in France, the Welsh and the Highland Scots in Britain, and the Irish in Ireland. The Republic of Ireland was already an independent country by this stage, but the historical tensions between the Irish, who traditionally spoke a Celtic language, and the English colonial regime were still there, and Ireland itself was, of course, neutral in World War II.

But was this scholarship in *Germanistik* and Celtic studies really entwined with the Nazi ideology, or was it just an opportunistic appeal to the interests of the regime in order to secure funding and political support?

CH: Well, I think the affinity was sincere. There's figures like Ludwig Mühlhausen, there's Leo Weisgerber, and Willy Krogmann. They had very deep affinities to this Celtic culture, and they were very hostile to what the British had done or were doing in Ireland. So I think there is a sincere element to it. There is also an opportunistic element if you look at Heinz Kloss, who was much more concerned with Germans, overseas Germans, or Germans outside the Reich, but he did get a lot of funding in relation to independent research institutes (*Forschungsstellen*).

Another way to look at this question is to look at the east. Michael Burleigh wrote a brilliant book called *Germany turns eastwards*, and it's about the scholarship of the predominantly Slavic east. What you can see there is a mixture, in policy terms, of getting people on board – so appropriating, assimilating – and also settler colonial ambitions. Some Ukrainians were working with the Nazis, and then you have the Latvian SS, you have collaboration, but in the long run, I guess there was a plan, for the whole of Europe, a mixture of ethnic states in the west and settler colonialism in the east.

How exactly that would have worked is unclear, but Alfred Rosenberg was saying to Hitler, "The Ukrainians hate Stalin." Rosenberg was from the east so he was familiar with the situation. And I think Hitler was, on the other hand, much more insistent on a kind of scorched earth policy because of this settler ambition. But they did have a European plan, and it did include a more "natural" ethnic ecology of Western Europe which would have been, I presume, ethnic states under Nazi tutelage, so sort of patron states.

Certainly, Leo Weisgerber was active in Brittany. And there was an attempt to use Flemish nationalism. Certainly in the case of the academics, they were sincerely interested in the project because they basically distrusted the modern state, the nation-state form, because it's not organic, but I think there was an overriding cynicism in the higher levels of the Nazi Party.

It wouldn't have been a great deal for the ethnic minorities in the end. The ruthlessness of it is such that the kind of autonomy they would have got would have been very, very thin. So again, I think the idea of drawing clean lines is underlying all of this, and the return to the organic state. But the academics didn't have the intellectual answers, really. And then there's the overriding technocratic, brutal nature of the project – which becomes stronger and stronger as the war goes on. This re-engineering project is secondary, I think, at a certain point because it's a brutal battle for survival.

But a lot of the academics are sincerely invested in these projects, so back to your original question, especially with the Celts, I think there are a lot of affinities, and the academic links went back way before the war, and they still continue, actually. There's still a Celtic Romanticism in Germany. It's nothing like it was, but I noticed that when I lived in Germany. There is this Romantic attachment to a particular form of Celtic imagery and way of being as opposed to the kind of hard capitalist modernity of England or the US. So I think that ethos remains – stripped, I should add, of its nasty toxic elements.

JMc: OK, so that brings us to the present day. Minority language rights are of course a major issue in mainstream linguistics today, but the focus today is perhaps on indigenous languages in places that have been subject to settler colonialism, such as North and South America and Australia, so the sort of project that Boas was engaged in back in these days. But also in Britain and France, the rights of speakers of Celtic languages are very much on the agenda and have managed to win some government support, and even in Germany, some small minorities such as the Sorbs in the Lausitz, in Brandenburg and Saxony, who speak a Slavic language, have been able to gain official support.

But today, minority language rights are usually considered a progressive issue, an effort to counteract the deleterious effects of colonialism and the aggressive spread of hegemonic cultures. How can an issue like this have such different, even diametrically opposed, political associations in different historical contexts?

CH: I think one of the keys to this is that the language minority politics of Europe between the wars and into the war is about territory. So the whole tension underlying it is the question, whose territory is this? And basically – back to the organic state – if you want to consolidate and survive and not to lose parts of your *Volk*, then it seems that you need political power in those regions in order to protect that.

Obviously, the Germans are hurting because they've lost a lot of territory and a lot of their speakers are now citizens of other states, so the whole issue is explosive at the level where people are going to be killed. To bring about this kind of ideal state, you're going to have to move people or kill them. So it's very different from the post-war US where it's an argument about cultural space or about legitimacy or access to social mobility. There's no underlying murderous potential to that, but of course there's a lot of social tension around it. So I think that's one difference.

I think that sociolinguistics has suffered from a single model of this, so if you say "mother tongue language rights", everyone goes, "Great!" Language politics should include politics. If you look at the politics of these states, it becomes a much more muddled and complicated story. Back in the 1990s, Robert Philipson would go around the world telling everyone to use their mother tongues – but he did it in English, of course – and in a way, it was a one-size-fits-all solution emanating from northern Europe. So my problem, in a way, is that we don't look enough at the actual politics, the real governmental system, the structures, the resourcing, and all the effects.

People can pat themselves on the back for saying, "I support language rights," but they don't actually cost it in any way, politically or economically. Maybe it's the problem with the identity left now that it's not interested in economics. You know, when I was young, Marxists and leftists would talk about economics all the time. Now, they only talk about identity, and it seems to me this is a problem for sociolinguistics.

The situation today is of course better in many ways, more progressive. Take the example of Welsh. Welsh is now enjoying quite a strong degree of official recognition, and that's great. I don't see any problem with that, and I think this can keep going further. But every speaker of Welsh is a native speaker of English as well, so it's a very unusual situation, and I think that's really beneficial to the kind of possibilities of this situation.

But in other situations, people are on the edge of these modern states, like in South America. It is a difficult issue. It's very easy to sit here and go, "They should keep their languages and cultures," but modernity can be brutal. The Welsh are in modernity, whereas in Brazil – or these Amazonian peoples – getting into modernity will destroy their cultures. I don't see any easy point of view from here.

Another huge block of states are the Leninist states or the former Leninist states, which is a vast percentage of the world population – so China, Vietnam, Laos, Burma to a degree, and even India, in a funny way – where you have official minority classifications centrally organized, and the politics of that are very, very different from the minority policies of, say, the US.

If we think back in the US context, both Uriel Weinrich and Joshua Fishman, in many ways the founders of modern sociolinguistics in the 1950s and '60s, have a whole list of Nazis in their references. I mean, not one or two, maybe 20 or 25. So how is that possible? Weinrich's *Languages in Contact*, if you look in the bibliography, there's a bunch of really nasty, toxic people there, one of whom was executed for war crimes. So how is that possible? It's because, well, one, I think in Fishman's case, he just was not interested in the problematic nature of minority politics in the interwar era, and he didn't understand Kloss, who was both his close collaborator and a former collaborator of the Nazis, and he was worried about protecting the program that he had, which was to promote ethnic revival in the US and globally in the decolonizing world, a kind of rational language politics or language engineering.

JMc: But your average sociolinguist – so someone like Weinreich or Fishman – who might be citing lots of Nazis, maybe their principle would be, don't say that they're hypocritical, say rather that they're apolitical – that the ideas are separate from the politics that they were used to support.

CH: Well, my theory with Weinreich was that he was trying to protect the discipline, and he did his fieldwork in Switzerland, so he was in the only bit of continental Europe which was still intact in some sense after the war, and I think he was such a straight and high-minded guy that he felt it beneath him to lay into these others.

But Max Weinreich, his father, wrote one of the first books on Nazi scholarship. And in his private correspondence, as Kalman Weiser showed in his 2018 paper, Max Weinreich was scathing about Franz Beranek, one of the Germans who worked on Yiddish. Max Weinreich called Beranek complicit in murder and so on. So there is something strange about that.

As for Fishman, it is possible he was protecting people. Or maybe he didn't know. I don't know whether it was Weinreich who gave him the references. Fishman certainly knew about Georg Schmidt-Rohr. Schmidt-Rohr had a complicated evolution: in 1932 he got into political trouble for seemingly suggesting that language could create *Volk*, and then he reoriented himself to get past the Nordicist attacks on him. But he was no liberal.

Then Fishman gradually stops citing German sources. In a way that's mapping the end of German dominance in academia after the war, and the rise of the US as the preeminent linguistics power.

JMc: What a claim to fame, preeminent linguistics power. It's not quite as impressive as being the greatest military power or economic power.

CH: True, but it goes together a little bit because look at the US university system, and then because of the expansion in the 1960s, American linguistics really took off. American sociolinguistics has a kind of virgin birth in the '60s. They act as if there was never a European background. There's something slightly odd about it, even though Kloss is there in meetings with leading figures in America like Dell Hymes and John J. Gumperz, and so on. They seem to forget all the literature from Britain – the British Empire was a key place for linguistic research – as well as all the material on the ethnic politics of Central and Eastern Europe. Sociolinguistics comes along and it's a very US thing.

JMc: That's probably a good note to end the interview on, so thank you very much for your answers to those questions.

CH: Thanks very much. It was good fun. I enjoyed that.

Primary sources

Boas, Franz. 1911a. *Handbook of American Indian languages.* Vol. 1. Washington, D.C.: Government Printing Office.

Boas, Franz. 1911b. *The mind of primitive man.* New York: Macmillan.

Fishman, Joshua. 1964. Language maintenance and language shift as a field of inquiry. *Linguistics* 2. 32–70.

Kloss, Heinz. 1941. *Brüder vor den Toren des Reiches. Vom volksdeutschen Schicksal.* Berlin: Hochmuth.

Mühlhausen, Ludwig. 1939. *Zehn irische Volkserzählungen aus Süd-Donegal, mit Übersetzung und Anmerkungen.* Halle: Niemeyer.

Philipson, Robert. 1992. *Linguistic imperialism.* Oxford: Oxford University Press.

Sapir, Edward. 1949. *Selected writings of Edward Sapir in language, culture and personality.* Los Angeles: University of California Press.

Schmidt-Rohr, Georg. 1932. *Die Sprache als Bildnerin der Völker. Eine Wesens- und Lebenskunde der Volkstümer.* Jena: Diederichs.

Schmidt-Rohr, Georg. 1933. *Mutter Sprache.* Jena: Diederichs.

Weinreich, Max. 1946. *Hitler's professors: The part of scholarship in Germany's crimes against the Jewish people.* New York: Yiddish Scientific Institute – Yivo.

Weinreich, Uriel. 1953. *Languages in contact: Findings and problems.* New York: Publications of the Linguistic Circle of New York.

Weisgerber, Johann Leo. 1939. *Die volkhaften Kräfte der Muttersprache.* 2nd ed. Frankfurt: Diesterweg.

Secondary sources

Burleigh, Michael. 1988. *Germany turns eastwards: A study of* Ostforschung *in the Third Reich.* Cambridge: Cambridge University Press.

Hutton, Christopher. 1999. *Linguistics and the Third Reich: Mother-tongue fascism, race and the science of language.* London: Routledge.

Hutton, Christopher. 2005. *Race and the Third Reich: Linguistics, racial anthropology and genetics in the dialect of* Volk. Cambridge: Polity.

Knobloch, Clemens. 2005. *Volkhafte Sprachforschung.* Tübingen: Niemeyer.

Weiser, Kalman. 2018. One of Hitler's professors: Max Weinreich and Solomin Birnbaum confront Franz Beranek. *Jewish Quarterly Review* 108. 106–124.

Chapter 10

The Copenhagen Circle

Lorenzo Cigana[a] & James McElvenny[b]

[a]University of Copenhagen [b]University of Siegen

JMc: Today we're talking about Louis Hjelmslev and the Copenhagen Linguistic Circle. To guide us through this topic, we're joined by Lorenzo Cigana, who is a researcher in the Department of Nordic Studies and Linguistics at the University of Copenhagen and currently undertaking a major project on the history of the Copenhagen Linguistic Circle.

So, Lorenzo, can you tell us, what was the Copenhagen Linguistic Circle? When was it around, who were the main figures involved, and what sort of scholarship did they pursue?

LC: Dear James, I guess the best way to put it is to say that the Copenhagen Linguistic Circle was among the most important and active centres in twentieth-century linguistic structuralism and language sciences, along with, of course, the Circles of Paris, Geneva, Prague and, on the other side of the Atlantic, New York. It has also been referred to as the Copenhagen School, but the suitability of this label is somewhat debatable.

Not just the existence of the Copenhagen Linguistic Circle, but its very structure, was actually tied to the structure of those similar organisations. It was founded by Louis Hjelmslev and Viggo Brøndal on the 24th of September 1931: that's almost exactly one month after the Second International Congress of Linguists, which was held between the 25th and the 29th of August 1931, in Geneva – a city that, of course, had symbolic value since it was the city in which Ferdinand de Saussure was born. And actually, if you check the pictures that were taken during the congress, you can see a lovely, merry company of linguists all

Lorenzo Cigana & James McElvenny. 2022. The Copenhagen Circle. In James McElvenny (ed.), *Interviews in the history of linguistics: Volume I*, 91–100. Berlin: Language Science Press. DOI: 10.5281/zenodo.7096306

queuing to visit Ferdinand de Saussure's mansion on the outskirts of the old part of the city. A very nice picture!

The Copenhagen Linguistic Circle also printed two series of proceedings. So we had *Bulletins*, the *Bulletin du Cercle linguistique de Copenhague*. The other was the *Travaux du Cercle linguistique de Copenhague*, which was a way to match what the Société linguistique de Paris and the Linguistic Circle of Prague were already doing at that time.

What about the internal organization, you asked. The circle was divided into scientific committees, each of them devoted to the discussion of specific topics. There was a glossematic committee, for instance, which was formed by Hjelmslev and Hans Jørgen Uldall, and tasked with the development of the theory called glossematics. Then there was a phonematics committee devoted to phonological analysis, and a grammatical committee which was focused on general grammar and morphology, which had a lot of momentum.

Now, you might have the impression here that it was Louis Hjelmslev who shaped the Circle, and you would be quite right: Louis Hjelmslev was definitely the leading figure. He was in many senses the engine behind the Circle's activity, something that he was actually reproached for in the following years.

At first, Hjelmslev got along very well with the other founder of the Circle, Viggo Brøndal. Hjelmslev was a comparative linguist and Indo-Europeanist, while Viggo Brøndal was a Romance philologist and philosopher, so they did complement each other. Moreover, they both were the descendants, so to speak, of two important academic traditions – something I'd really like to draw attention to, as in fact it is important to bear in mind that the Circle didn't come out of the blue. The sprout had deep roots.

Hjelmslev had been a student of Otto Jespersen and Holger Pedersen. Now, the first, Otto Jespersen, was an internationally renowned and influential linguist. He was said to be one of the greatest language scholars of the nineteenth and twentieth centuries, and his research was focused on grammar and the English language. He wrote a number of important works in syntax, like the theory of the three ranks. He also wrote wide-ranging contributions on the philosophy of linguistics, such 'The Logic of Language' (*Sprogets logik*) in 1913 and the *Philosophy of Grammar* in 1924. This is coincidentally what I like to call my domain of research, philosophy of grammar. Holger Pedersen, in turn, was a pure Indo-Europeanist and was in the same generation of Vilhelm Thomsen, Karl Verner – who is often mistakenly taken as German – and Hermann Möller, who corresponded with Ferdinand de Saussure and offered his version of the laryngeal theory. Although less interested in general linguistics, Pedersen worked on Albanian, Celtic, Tocharian, and Hittite, and postulated the existence of a Nostratic macro-family, linking the Indo-European family to others, like Finno-Ugric and Altaic.

Let us take a look at Viggo Brøndal: what was his background? He was a pupil of Harald Høffding, one of the most important Danish philosophers, who worked extensively on the notion of analogy and analogical thinking, which was a topic of great importance in the epistemology of that time. Moreover, he read and commented on the *Course in general linguistics*, the *Cours de linguistique générale*, of Saussure, as soon as it was published, and was particularly receptive to all that came from Wilhelm von Humboldt, Gottfried Wilhelm von Leibniz, and from the phenomenological tradition of Franz Brentano and Edmund Husserl.

However, if we look even further back, we see that the scholars I have just mentioned – Jespersen, Høffding and Pedersen – were in turn standing on the shoulders of other giants. And in fact they all had knowledge, in one way or another, of the work of their predecessors, notably Johan Madvig and Rasmus Rask, who both lived in the early nineteenth century.

Let us just focus on Rask, who is rightly considered as the pioneer or the founding father of multiple linguistic disciplines, like Indo-European linguistics and Iranian philology, among others. Yet Rask didn't just make factual contributions to language comparison, but also insightful theoretical and methodological advances. These advances can be found in his lectures on the philosophy of language and were especially dear to Louis Hjelmslev, who saw in them an anticipation of his own approach, and it's no wonder why. Rask distinguished between two complementary stances in linguistics: the mechanical perspective, which provides a collection of facts, and a philosophical perspective, which tries to find the system or the link between all these facts. Rask described the difference between these two perspectives in the following way. The mechanical view deals with the process of making the materials required to paint a portrait: the colors, the canvas, etc. But only the philosophical perspective deals with the process of painting and the study of portraits themselves. This distinction is quite important.

The reason why I decided to give this glimpse into the background of the Circle is that it is important to bear in mind that the influence of those figures lingered on: they were still present in the mind of the Circle's members as a tradition they all came from. Rask in particular was dear to many linguists of the Copenhagen School. Jespersen wrote a biography of Rask, Hjelmslev collected his diaries and tried to make him a structuralist *ante litteram*, and Diderichsen tried to reframe Hjelmslev's own interpretations. It was on such fertile ground that the Copenhagen Linguistic Circle built its own scholarship.

Let's now return to the Copenhagen School itself. You asked, James, who its members were and what kind of contribution they made. Well, despite the claim that each member built their own tradition, there were indeed some shared projects, glossematics being one of them, possibly the most important. The work of building this new theory, glossematics, was carried out mostly, of course, by Louis Hjelmslev and his friend and colleague Hans Jørgen Uldall, who joined his project in 1934.

Now, we have already spoken about Louis Hjelmslev, but very little is known about Hans Jørgen Uldall, who was a remarkable figure in his own right. He was first and foremost a very talented phonetician and collaborated with Daniel Jones, who was arguably the greatest British phonetician of the twentieth century. Uldall's phonetic transcriptions were also known to be extremely precise, and yet he was also trained as a field anthropologist, another interesting aspect of his life. He travelled all across America, especially around California, carrying out research for Franz Boas. This gave him an incredible background that complemented Louis Hjelmslev's own strong comparative and epistemological approach very well.

Of Hjelmslev and Uldall's collaboration during the 1930s, it was reported that they couldn't say where one person's ideas finished and the other's started. I really believe this is such a brilliant example of collaboration between two scholars. But of course, there were also other members. If you take the proceedings of the Sixth International Congress of Linguists, for example, which was held in Paris in 1949, you can find a nice summary of the activity of the Copenhagen Circle since its very foundation. It's a very informative summary, because it gives a clear idea about how the circle understood itself, or rather, how it wanted to present itself to the audience. Its motto sounded like: "We deal with general grammar and morphology over everything else".

Hjelmslev worked on the internal structure of morphological categories: case, pronouns, articles, and so forth. Brøndal, too, in a way: he was trying to describe the structural nature of such systems and their variability as two complementary aspects connected to logical levels of semantic nature. But then there were also Paul Diderichsen, Knud Togeby, Jens Holt, and Hans Christian Sørensen, four fascinating figures.

If we look at Knud Togeby, he is probably the best known of these four, at least beyond the borders of Denmark. He wrote *La structure immanente de la langue française* in 1951, a kind of compendium in which he described French in all its layers, from grammar to phonology, and was harshly criticized by Martinet. If you pay attention to the way Togeby used the very term "immanent", *structure immanente de la langue française*, you'll recognize the imprint of Hjelmslev: after all, it was Hjelmslev that stressed the need of an immanent description in the first place.

Paul Diderichsen was originally a pupil of Brøndal, and became a follower of Hjelmslev only later. He is mostly known for having developed the so-called fields theory, which is basically a valency model for syntax that works particularly well for Germanic languages and that played a big role in how Danish was analysed – and how it is still analysed today. He also developed what he called graphematics, which means a description of written language in conformity with the framework of glossematics, since it was based on graphemes conceived as formal units. However, Diderichsen became frustrated with this system and cast it aside.

Then we have Jens Holt and Hans Christian Sørensen, two figures that I personally feel very close to. They were both comparative linguists; they both struggled with Hjelmslev's theory while trying to apply it to the morphological category of aspect, and they both ended up reworking some points of Hjelmslev's theory in their own ways. For instance, Jens Holt tried to develop his own "rational semantics" – and here again we find this strange urge to qualify a theory as rational, something that tells us a lot about the general epistemological posture taken back then. He called his model "pleremics" – that is, an investigation of content entities in plain reference to glossematics, which was indeed its natural framework.

Finally, we should mention Eli-Fischer Jørgensen, who cannot be left out of the picture. We can think of her as the Danish version of Lady Welby, the glue of the Circle. She corresponded with the most important figures of linguistics and phonetics at that time, and had a life-long correspondence with Roman Jakobson. She began her studies in syntax but found it too philosophical, so she decided to change, landing in phonology and phonetics instead.

Now, despite the consonances between the members, and despite their ties to Hjelmslev, no school as such was established, no consistent tradition. They were all tapping into Louis Hjelmslev's ideas, but they did that according to their own needs, as glossematics was the most consistent theory discussed back then. Yet because of (or perhaps thanks to) their different backgrounds, they could keep their own stances and views about linguistics and glossematics too. That must have been a source of some discomfort for Hjelmslev himself later on, to have his theory modified in various ways to suit different ends.

JMc: How did the Copenhagen Circle relate to other linguistic schools active at this time, in particular the Prague Linguistic Circle?

LC: In order to answer your second question, we will use the strategy that was developed by Homer in the Iliad. You know, portraying in poetic terms the clash between two whole armies is a hell of a job. Homer's trick to describe the war between the two armies, the Greeks and the Trojans, was to collapse the armies into champions. So instead of having complicated, confused war scenes, we have battle scenes between two champions. This is what I would like to do here, because it was actually … well, I would not call it a war, but a conflict to be sure, in a way. That was really what happened back then.

The Prague Circle and the Copenhagen Circle had a relationship that could be called a friendly competition, or perhaps a competitive friendship. This doesn't characterize the attitude of every single member of the two circles, but if we boil it down to the relationship between our main actors or "champions", as I suggested – namely Roman Jakobson, Nikolai Trubetzkoy, Viggo Brøndal and Louis Hjelmslev – the label is pretty accurate.

Let us take, for instance, what happened at the Second Congress of Phonetic Sciences in London in 1935. The backstory for it is that they had all met at the First International Congress of Linguists in the Hague, in 1928, so they knew each other. Then around 1932, Jakobson – or rather, the Prague Circle – would write to Hjelmslev asking, "Wouldn't you be interested in providing a phonological description of modern Danish?" To which Hjelmslev answered, "Yeah, I can do that." Then two years passed, Hjelmslev met Uldall, they discovered that both the content and the expression side of language – roughly, the signified and the signifier – could be described in parallel, so their approach changed somewhat, and in 1934, Hjelmslev wrote to Uldall saying, "You know what? We are not going to give what Jakobson asked us for. We will give our own talks, and put forward our own theory." That theory was "phonematics", the first sprout of glossematics, still centered on the expression plane. "Let us show them that we are a battalion, that *wir marschieren.*" And I am quoting here.

All this – mind you – happened at the very heart of the Second International Congress of Phonetic Sciences (London 1935), and at the very same session in which Trubetzkoy was speaking. It must have been quite disruptive, it must have looked like a sort of a declaration of war. And it was certainly understood as such, given that Trubetzkoy himself wrote to Jakobson wondering whether Hjelmslev was a friend to the phonological cause or rather an enemy.

As you know, in the past we have probably been a little bit too keen in considering this kind of competition on a personal level, as if between Trubetzkoy and Hjelmslev there was a personal animosity or rancour. I personally do not think so, or rather, if it was so, it was because scientific contrasts were felt in a very serious way, as back then it was of paramount importance to gauge one's commitment to a common cause, namely the building of a new discipline – structural linguistics.

Indeed, starting from 1935, Hjelmslev and Uldall put a lot of effort into disseminating their view, stressing the fact that it was complementary and not identical to the one that the Prague Circle was developing. Hence, for instance, the stress that Hjelmslev put on the fact that research into phonology should focus on the possible pronunciations of linguistic elements and not be limited to the concrete or the factual ("realized") pronunciation.

Their view on language was becoming ever broader, and correspondingly, their frustration grew, too. In the same years, around 1935–1936, Hjelmslev was invited by Alan Ross to give lectures on his new science in Leeds in Great Britain, and after sensing the rather sceptical attitude in the audience, Hjelmslev wrote back to Uldall saying, "No one seems to understand what we are trying to do. They all want old traditional Neogrammarian phonetics. Oh, Uldall, I really want to go back to the continent."

A rich ground for confrontation between the different approaches was the theory of distinctive features, or *mérismes*, as Benveniste would have called them. Prague was keen on analysing a phoneme into smaller features of a phonetic nature, while for Hjelmslev, this procedure was too hasty. If phonemes are of an abstract, formal nature, they should be analysed further into formal elements rather than straight into phonetic features. Such basic formal elements were called glossemes and represent the very goal of glossematics, which was accordingly called the science of glossemes, the basic invariants of a language. And then there was, of course, the aspect of markedness and binarism. This is the idea which Jakobson stubbornly maintained throughout his life, that distinctive features always occur in pairs defined by logical opposition, an idea that Hjelmslev never endorsed and actually actively fought.

So overall, I think one could say that the relationship between these approaches – Prague versus Copenhagen and Paris – was twofold. Viewed from the outside, they gave the idea of being a uniform approach, a single front opposed to the one of traditional grammar or traditional linguistics of the past. They were indeed trying to build what Hjelmslev hoped for: a new classicism. However, viewed from the inside – if we increase, so to speak, the focus of our lens – we begin to notice massive differences that might appear a matter of detail, but that are quite significant in themselves. We have, at the same time, both unity and diversity, a key aspect that needs to be taken into account if you want to give an accurate picture of what happened in structural linguistics back then.

JMc: What became of the Copenhagen Circle? Did it continue over several generations, or does it have a contained, closed history with a clear endpoint? What lasting effects did the scholarship of the Copenhagen Linguistic Circle have on linguistics?

LC: Well, the Copenhagen Linguistic Circle is still alive and kicking, actually. It has changed direction somewhat, and we may say that the structural approach or the structural generation has flowed into the new generation, which has a functional orientation. But this would be to oversimplify the state of affairs. I do believe the flow from one generation to the other wasn't a matter of simple acknowledgement or rejection of approaches, methods, and ideas.

The modern approach, the functional one, understands itself as having some continuity with the broad framework of structuralism, even of glossematics. Yet in many respects, the modern framework is also a reaction against the purely formal stance that glossematic structuralism represented in Copenhagen, as well as with Hjelmslev's somewhat oversized figure not just in scholarship and intellectual activity, but also in academic bureaucracy. It is, after all, a game of positions, of theoretical postures. Some of them can be seen as interpretation or explanations of previous positions. Others are original claims that are not necessarily linked with the previous theories.

I should mention first of all that functionalism in linguistics can be seen as sort of a combination of insights coming from the structural framework, with the addition of some ideas that were developed later on, especially by Simon Dik in Amsterdam, and also with some ideas coming from cognitivism.

At the very core of Danish functionalism, even if it may be trivial to mention it, is the attention given to how linguistic elements are used in given contexts. So in functionalism, it's how they function, or what is functional in a given context, that matters. In this perspective, thus, "function" has little to do with the notion of "relation", which was the key notion used by Hjelmslev. So here we have the first difference between "old structuralism" and functionalism: "function" in terms of relation was what linguistic structuralism and Hjelmslev's approach wanted to use. In the new context of functionalism, "function" is rather interpreted as a role, and it is strongly tied to the idea of language as a communicative tool.

This is very interesting, because such a definition may appear so obvious and trivial, right? Language as communication. But actually, this is not. After all, this was not how language was conceived in other structural contexts. For Hjelmslev, but to some extent to Uldall, and possibly to many other structuralists, too, the point was not communication, but formation or articulation. According to this hypothesis, language is a way to communicate only because it is in the first place a tool to articulate meanings in relation to expressions and vice versa. It's also a way to represent subjectivity as such, a position that was explained so well by Oswald Ducrot, for instance, and which is echoed in Cassirer.

So, claiming that language serves to communicate can be seen as a position that was held in reaction to what a certain structural tradition was trying to do, and this entails some other theoretical consequences, like how expression and content – so signifier and signified – were interpreted and are interpreted nowadays, a cascade of differences and of conceptual claims that may seem a matter of details, once again, but which we need to be aware of.

I cannot elaborate further on this point without entering into details, but let me just say that these differences are not just terminological. How function and form are defined in linguistics nowadays is not how they were defined back then, so we cannot assume these concepts are universal, or trivial, or commonsensical. Not at all. The task of a language scientist is also to draw attention to these epistemological stances, since they have a deep influence on his or her work, and this is, I think, the best way to understand our job, too, and a nice way to update what Saussure felt himself about the urge to show what linguists do. This is why I don't particularly like the label "historiography of linguistics". I prefer something like "comparative epistemology" because this is actually what we do. So I hope to have answered your question, James. Thank you once again.

JMc: Yeah, that was great. Thanks very much.

Primary sources

Bulletin du Cercle Linguistique de Copenhague 1941–1965 (8–31). Choix de commu-nications et d'interventions au débat lors des séances tenues entre septembre 1941 et mai 1965. 1941–1965. Copenhagen: Akademisk Forlag.
Bulletins du Cercle Linguistique de Copenhague. 1931–1940. Vol. 1–7.
Diderichsen, Paul. 1960. *Rasmus Rask og den grammatiske tradition: Studier over vendepunktet i sprogvidenskabens historie.* Copenhagen: Munskgaard.
Hjelmslev, Louis. 1931–1935. *Rasmus Rask. Udvalgte Afhandlinger udgivet paa Bekostning af Rask-ørsted Fondet i Hundredaaret for Rasks Død paa Foranled-ning af Vilhelm Thomsen af Det danske Sprog- og Litteraturselskab ved Louis Hjelmslev med inledning af Holger Petersen.* Vol. 1–3. Copenhagen: Levin & Munksgaards.
Holt, Jens. 1946. *Rationel semantik (pleremik).* Copenhagen: Munksgaards.

Jespersen, Otto. 1913. *Sprogets logik (The logic of language)*. Copenhagen: Schultz.

Jespersen, Otto. 1918. *Rasmus Rask: i hundredåret efter hans hovedvaerk*. Gyldendal: Schultz.

Jespersen, Otto. 1924. *Philosophy of grammar*. London: Allen & Unwin.

Rapport sur l'activité du Cercle Linguistique de Copenhague 1931–1951. 1951. Copenhagen: Nordisk Sprog- og Kulturforlag.

Saussure, Ferdinand de. 1922 [1916]. *Cours de linguistique générale*. Charles Bally & Albert Sechehaye (eds.). 2nd ed. Paris: Payot.

Travail collectif du Cercle linguistique de Copenhague. 1949. In *Proceedings of the Sixth International Congress of Linguists*, 126–135. Paris: Klincksieck.

Secondary sources

Cigana, Lorenzo & Frans Gregersen (eds.). 2022. *Structure as one – structure as many. Studies in structuralism*. Copenhagen: Det Kongelige Dankse Videskabernes Selskab.

Ducrot, Oswald. 1968. *Le structuralisme en linguistique*. Paris: Éditions du Seuil.

Rasmussen, Michael. 1987. Hjelmslev et Brøndal. Rapport sur un différend. *Langages* 86. 41–58.

Thomas, Margaret. 2019. *Formalism and functionalism in linguistics. The engineer and the collector*. London: Routledge.

Lightning Source UK Ltd.
Milton Keynes UK
UKHW032217260922
409489UK00004B/119